INSIDE THE
ORGANIC
CHURCH

ALSO BY BOB WHITESEL

GROWTH BY ACCIDENT, DEATH BY PLANNING
How NOT To Kill a Growing Congregation

STAYING POWER
Why People Leave the Church Over Change
(And What You Can Do About It!)

A HOUSE DIVIDED
Bridging the Generation Gaps in Your Church
with Kent R. Hunter

INSIDE THE ORGANIC CHURCH

Learning from 12 Emerging Congregations

Bob Whitesel

Abingdon Press / Nashville

INSIDE THE ORGANIC CHURCH
LEARNING FROM 12 EMERGING CONGREGATIONS

Copyright © 2006 by Abingdon Press

This book is printed on acid-free paper.

Library of Congress Cataloging-in-Publication Data

Whitesel, Bob.
    Inside the organic church : learning from 12 emerging congregations / Bob Whitesel.
        p. cm.
    Includes bibliographical references.
    ISBN 0-687-33116-1 (binding: pbk., adhesive : alk. paper)
    1. Generation X—Religious life. 2. Generation Y—Religious life. 3. Church work with young adults. 4. Public worship. I. Title.

    BV4529.2.W45 2006
    259.084'2—dc22

                                                                                2006005202

06 07 08 09 10 11 12 13 14 15—10 9 8 7 6 5 4 3 2 1

MANUFACTURED IN THE UNITED STATES OF AMERICA

CONTENTS & INSIGHTS

CHAPTER 1
St. Thomas' Church, Sheffield, England 1
    1. Cluster small groups to maximize effectiveness.
    2. Use symbols and icons for retention and comprehension
       of important spiritual truths.
    3. If your church averages over 125 adults each weekend,
       employ unity events to maintain cohesiveness.

CHAPTER 2
the sol café, Edmonton, Alberta, Canada 13
    1. Let worship emerge from your ambiance.
    2. Use self-sustaining venues, realizing profitability may
       sustain the venue but probably not pastoral staff.
    3. It helps when a missional church can face its mission
       field.

CHAPTER 3

  1. Encourage participation in small groups to retain intimacy, accountability, and mission.
  2. If feasible, look for underutilized or vacant mid-sized malls as potential church facilities.
  3. Use technologically up-to-date tools such as short DVDs to communicate truth.

CHAPTER 4

  1. Balance both the cultural and the evangelistic mandates.
  2. The cultural mandate must be carefully studied and replicated, not only because of its strategic importance, but also because evangelicals lack proficiency.
  3. Concerted effort will be required to keep the two mandates in balance, even among the organic church.

CHAPTER 5

  1. Let sacred spaces support your mission.
  2. Engage and mentor artists of varied mediums.
  3. Create multigenerational (Multi-gen.) communities.

CHAPTER 6

  1. Carefully investigate and examine elements of a culture.
  2. Sift happens! Sift elements of a culture.
  3. Reject or affirm elements of a culture.

CHAPTER 7

  1. Balance an *ancient-future* orientation to reach people who appreciate liturgical expressions.
  2. Use organic involvement (such as many voices) in the creation of your liturgical expressions.
  3. Build your persuasion upon proclamation and presence.

2. Learn to "improv."
3. Release your innovation gene.

THE FINALE

Conclusions

Why Commence with a Finale?

In this book I have chosen several unique constructions, of which musical metaphors, the image of a journey, and an inaugural Finale are but three. I must admit, there are several reasons why my penchant for unfamiliar constructs is an outgrowth of my unpredictable yet exhilarating travels through what has been called the emerging church.

Commencing this book with a finale serves a purpose I learned from these youthful congregations: tell me the direction of your travels before you ask me to accompany you. And thus, this epilogue tenders a rearward glance over my journey and proposes some core conclusions.

Musical metaphors also seemed fitting expressions for my journey through these young Christian congregations. This term emerged as fitting as I sought to describe congregations that were brimming with a fusion of ideas, innovations, and originality.

The concept of a journey was a final construct that helped fuse into a cohesive record my exploration of these twelve congregations. The concept of a journey helped convey that though I experienced a nexus with these young congregations, I am still an outsider, a temporary visitor living among them to understand them, but never truly native.

Subsequently, these youthful congregations taught me that mixing things up and challenging expectations is a good way to aid in retention. Therefore, to keep this journey from becoming a stale travelogue and to aid in retention, I have embraced a number of innovations. The use of musical terminology, travel imagery, and conclusions at the onset are the first the reader will encounter.

What Is an Emerging Church?

An emerging congregation is an appellation attached to churches populated largely by young adults under the age of thirty. Though attendees and especially leaders may be over thirty, an ability to effectively reach out to those under thirty years of age characterizes these congregations. A self-applied label, this term connotes perceived parallels with the so-called emerging post-modern philosophy of the twentieth century. Although a fuller explanation of postmodernity will wait for our prologue, suffice it to say that emerging churches are a branch of Christian expression created and led by young people.

In the forthcoming section "Prelude," I will explain why a more fitting appellation may be the "organic church," for "emerging" connotes something that is intensifying, and this may not always be the case. However, for simplicity, I will use the term "emerging organic church," or just "organic church."

Where Did the Emerging Organic Church Come From?

To understand the organic church's roots, a few definitions are in order.

Generation X, according to the nineteen-year demarcations preferred by sociologists, is the generation born between 1965 and 1983. Generation Xers grew up under the influence of their baby boomer parents, the Internet, computers, and a multimedia barrage. Their parents, the boomers, one of the largest generations birthed in the Western world, resulted from an upswing, or boom, in births following World War II. Born between 1946 and 1964, boomers have enjoyed a life of unparalleled prosperity and influence. But, not surprising, their children have cast a critical and unsympathetic eye toward the failure of their parents' quest to unite prosperity with spiritual (and emotional) peace.

Perhaps in reaction, boomers applied the nihilistic label Generation X to their offspring. Intended possibly to denote a disparagement of Generation X's penchant for criticism and skepticism, the term Generation X has come to describe a generation that does not readily, nor uncritically, embrace the structures and strategies of their parents.

Subsequently, Generation X has cast an analytical eye toward the evangelical boomer church of their parents, finding it lacking in an ability to unite spiritual, global, and emotional peace. An outgrowth of this appears to be a desire to remake all things boomer into structures and styles more authentic and compassionate. Generation X has labeled these experiments in adapting Christian methodology to a post-Christian, post-modern world: the emerging church.

While visiting these organic congregations, an Old Testament story kept coming to mind. The book of Daniel tells the story of Babylonian king Belshazzar, whose kingdom, for all of its might and prestige, had birthed a hollow and shallow spirituality. Chapter 5, verses 5-25, tell us that while Belshazzar was reveling in his power and influence, a hand mysteriously appeared on the wall scrawling the cryptic phrase *"Mene, Mene, Tekel, Parsin."* Only when translated by Daniel did the content of the admonition become clear: "MENE, God has numbered the days of your kingdom and brought it to an end; TEKEL, you have been weighed on the scales and found wanting; PERES, your kingdom is divided and given to the Medes and Persians" (Daniel 5:26-28 NRSV). Perhaps in disbelief, perhaps in uncertainty, Belshazzar did little; and that night, an alliance of Medes and Persians breached the walls of the city, looting and razing the pride of Babylon.

The lesson often drawn from this story is that God is not only a loving and compassionate, but also an analytical and a methodical deity, expecting effort (Matthew 25:24-30), outcomes (Matthew 28:19-20), and authentic spirituality (John 4:23-24). And though from human vantages society's accolades and opulence are often synonymous with God's approval, in reality they may not be.[1]

Not surprising, in organic churches, Generation X often seems to be conducting an appraisal of boomer ritual, traditions, worldviews, and spirituality. And in my conversations with attendees of these young churches, I find a general attitude that mirrors that of the hand on Belshazzar's wall: "the boomer church has been found wanting."

Accordingly, I have noted an inclination in the organic church toward experimentation and innovation as a means to improve ineffective forms of retention and ritual that Generation X have experienced in their parents' churches. Thus, their organic worship celebrations are awash with unique and innovative rituals and configurations. To the uninitiated they may seem at the very least unorthodox, and at the most, profane. But, at their core I have found these constructs primarily experiments toward the goal, held in common with their boomer progenitors, to more fully experience God and his power and to communicate this more authentically with outsiders.

Where Does This Journey Go (and Where Might It Lead You)?

The Melodies and Rhythms of the Organic Church

Within the organic church there are several fundamental and prevalent attitudes, and I will describe these shortly in the musical vernacular as "melodies."

However, these attitudes are usually so tailored, so customized to each church's unique environment and mission that an "uncommon" construct is in order, further describing them. Thus, in this book I have labeled the localized versions of these foundational attitudes as "rhythms." This term was chosen because these viewpoints are similar to musical rhythms, for I encountered each in varied forms, cadences, and volumes in each organic congregation. Thus, although the foundational musical score is generally the same, each emerging congregation creates its own musical stylings or "rhythms" of these foundational melodies.

However, below I have identified four rhythmic underpinnings, that is to say, foundational attitudes or melodies, that provide the musical score or tune behind all of these organic rhythms. Thus, take these following observations as underlying musical scores from which many churches can vary the tempo, pulse, beat, or rhythm to indigenize the lessons of the emerging church to a church's historical context and personality.

Four Melodies Behind the Organic Church

Below are four consistent melodic patterns that I have witnessed repeatedly in the underpinnings of organic churches. The rationale and applicability of these melodies will come out more coherently as the reader plies the case studies in this volume. However, for each melody I will tender a short introductory explanation.

(1) The Melody of Orthodoxy

Much of the criticism about the emerging organic church has focused upon worries and reservations that, due to their engagement with postmodern philosophies, organic churches may subtly begin to embrace heretical beliefs.

Quite frankly, before I embarked upon my journey I had a premonition that I would find a proliferation of unorthodox theology. Although I did find some congregations that embraced elements of nonorthodox Christianity,[2] I was surprised to find this not to be widespread in the emerging organic church. The vast majority of my encounters were with orthodox theology, coupled with denominational predilections. Thus, while in these churches the methodology is experimental, entrepreneurial, and inventive, their theology usually follows quite closely orthodox and denominational roots.

For example, while attending The Bridge in Tempe, Arizona, I found the theology and key worship elements very much in keeping with their traditional Southern Baptist theology and practice. This even though the church was meeting in the very un–Southern Baptist venue of a college nightclub. Again, at St. Thomas' Church in Sheffield, England, I found a very pervasive Anglican theology and membership ritual, even though their worship styles and management structures were radical departures from Anglican expectations. At Bluer, a Minneapolis congregation affiliated with the Vineyard Movement, consistent Vineyard theology was evident in both the sermon and the songs even though the latter were overlaid with generous doses of musical experimentation and liturgical innovation. Still again, at the Sol Café in Edmonton, Alberta, I found a consistent and pervasive Christian and Missionary Alliance theology, emerging by their own admission from their denominational roots.

Granted, there are many organic congregations that have, in their interaction with postmodern culture, embraced elements that are not orthodox and perhaps even aberrant. However, to my surprise, the majority of these emerging congregations have adopted the theology and core beliefs of the denominations that birthed them.[3]

We shall see later that herein lies an important lesson for the church; that the theological milieu in which an organic church is birthed persists as a powerful predicator and guide to future theological behavior.

(2) The Melody of Authenticity
(A Course Correction for the Boomer Church)

Another prevalent melody, like those that recur in your head with unwelcome frequency, was the reminder that Generation X leaders view boomer churches as having sacrificed authentic spiritual encounter on the altar of professionalism and perfection.

"You don't understand McGavran at all,"[4] stated a red-faced and undoubtedly frustrated young man in Sheffield, England. "McGavran was about building bridges with people who don't go to church," he continued. "Your churches want professional music so you can build roads to other Christians. You're losing the heart of worship and just trading sheep."

I took subtle, yet concealed, offense to my perceived lack of appreciation for Donald A. McGavran, who had first talked so passionately about "church growth" and "building bridges" to unchurched people. I had studied under McGavran's protégés C. Peter Wagner, Win Arn, Eddie Gibbs, George Hunter, and others. And in some circles I was regarded as a modern interpreter of McGavran's concepts. But on this day, I represented the boomer church leadership. And the veracity of this young man's comments reminded me that the grey flecks in my hair, which to some represent erudition, to this young man only represent a target.

As soon as I got my ego in check, I was able to appreciate the tenor of his annoyance. Growing up in a small evangelical yet boomer church in England, he had seen the desire for perfection and professionalism erode his search for an authentic spiritual encounter. "It seems the pastor was more concerned about feedback from the microphones than about experiencing God," he lamented. "We had meetings every Monday about what went wrong on Sunday. But we never had meetings on how to connect with God on Sunday. It was like the expectation was that if boomers get everything perfect, then the Holy Spirit will show up. I don't need that pressure. And it doesn't work."

He was right. As a church consultant I had experienced that same attitude at countless boomer churches. And I, too, disdained those environs in which performance or professionalism detracted from the heart of worship. These malfunctions were too prevalent in the boomer church, and this young man had noticed it.

Not surprising, many of these emerging organic congregations speak of seeking "authenticity" in their worship encounters. Authenticity is a term that juxtaposes the difference between authentic encounter and prefab worship.

Subsequently, a pervasive disdain for programs transplanted from large successful churches also runs throughout these organic churches. Although many programs and strategies are useful for fostering spiritual health, an uncritical implementation without regard to the personality of the local church has soured many young leaders. This to them seems to be inauthentic, simply crossbreeding generic programming.[5]

Herein lies another lesson for boomer leaders, that Generation X will evaluate you not upon your outward successes, but upon the authenticity of spiritual, holistic, and indigenized endeavors.

(3) The Melody of Engagement: Social and Spiritual

Engagement is the practice of initializing contact between two or more entities. In addition, engagement is a good description of how the church should foster contact with unchurched individuals in a way that allows the Holy Spirit and the Word of God to bring about social and spiritual change. Simply, this is the mission of Christian engagement: both spiritual and cultural redemption.

Biblical texts supporting spiritual redemption through faith in Jesus Christ are pervasive. Matthew 7:7-14, Matthew 28:19-20, Luke 4:18-19, John 3:16, John 4:34-35, Romans 6:23, and Romans 10:9-10 are just a few of the scriptures that provide a starting place for understanding Jesus' redemptive work. This work has come to be known as the "evangelistic mandate."

Redemption from societal inequities is also described in the Bible. Just a few of the scriptures that can provide an enlightening side trip are the Great Commandment of Matthew 22:37-39, Luke 3:11-14, Luke 6:20, and James 1:27. Arthur Glasser, who succeeded McGavran as the dean of the Fuller School of World Mission, polarized the term "cultural mandate" as a description of this admonition, and to parallel it with the more well-known "evangelistic mandate."[6] Peter Wagner gave one of the best descriptions of the cultural mandate as "distribution of wealth, the balance of nature, marriage and the family, human government, keeping the peace, cultural integrity, liberation of the oppressed—

these and other global responsibilities rightly fall within the cultural mandate."[7] Even more succinctly, Billy Graham said, "Jesus taught that we are to take regeneration in one hand and a cup of cold water in the other."[8]

Few would argue with the centrality of the spiritual and social redemption of humankind. But despite Billy Graham's pithy observation, in reality, few local churches are good at balancing both.[9] All too typically churches focus on one or the other of these biblical mandates. And as a result, churches are often viewed by outsiders, as well as by insiders, as one-sided, deficient in a wholistic strategy. Thus, a perceived inequitable bias by boomer churches toward spiritual engagement over social engagement is a driving force behind organic church endeavors to become engaged both spiritually *and* socially.[10]

The inequality in the way the boomer church practices these dual mandates rouses and agitates Generation X. Donald McGavran warned of this in his classic volume, *Understanding Church Growth,* stating,

> Today the sinfulness of the social order offends thoughtful Christians everywhere. . . . The great inequalities of wealth and poverty among the haves and have-nots, and the revolting treatment meted out to oppressed minorities, are clearly contrary to the will of the God and Father of our Lord Jesus Christ.[11]

Not surprising, I have found a thunderous and strident melody of indignation echoing through emerging congregations birthed in a frustration that most boomer churches have been unable successfully to address the cultural mandate, and thus strike a balance in meeting spiritual and physical needs.

(4) The Melody of Missional Church Growth

Finally, I discovered that a recurring melody within the emerging church is a desire to revisit classic church growth understanding. While talking to the lead pastor of Bluer, we discussed John Wimber, a founder of the Vineyard Movement and a campaigner for church growth. "The Vineyard Movement has been so many things," he began. "Signs and wonders, the Brownsville revival, the Toronto Blessing. But I want to return to the basics of what it means to understand how God grows his church," recounted John Musick. "It [the Vineyard Movement] has become so many things since the time of Wimber, but we have to go back to the basics of why the Vineyard started; it was to understand and discover church growth. I want to be more Vineyard than Vineyards are today."

Over four thousand miles away, the same appreciation for church growth echoed inside the massive stone walls of St. Thomas' Church in Sheffield, England. There, too, a recovery of church growth principles had driven the church uniquely to structure their church for growth. "Church growth needs to be recovered," said Mick Woodhead. "Not in its bizarre fringe forms, but in its simplicity and straightforwardness that helps churches grow." A discussion of St. Tom's strategic insights are covered in chapter 1.

In many of my conversations with these organic leaders, classic church growth understandings as elucidated by McGavran, Wagner, Gibbs, Arn, Hunter, and others surfaced. However, few books since these early volumes were widely lauded by organic leaders, except for one. The seminal tome that many young leaders thought captured the core values of classic church growth was *Missional Church,* edited by Darrell Guder.[12]

Guder, et al. make the argument that the church in the West has come to think of itself as residing within a Christian culture. However, Guder and his colleagues argue that "rather than occupying a central and influential place, North American Christian churches are increasingly marginalized, so much so that in our urban areas they represent a minority movement. It is by now a truism to speak of North America as a mission field."[13] With lucid and forceful arguments, these writers expose the church in the West as neither esteemed nor shaping culture, but rather derided and distained by modern culture. Anglican bishop Lesslie Newbigin had forewarned of this trend in 1984, when he argued that while the West had once been a Christendom society, it was now clearly post-Christian, if not anti-Christian.[14]

It is this keen awareness of a post-Christian, even antichurch culture that drives the ideology and strategies of the emerging organic church. And they embrace, as does Guder, a belief that the only solution for survival is for the church to begin to think of itself as a "missionary" organization within an unsympathetic cultural milieu.

Guder labels this a "missional" understanding of the church's mission and models. In very simplistic terms it can be described as the following: in a missional church you will not have an evangelism department, because all consider themselves part of the mission by way of whatever careers they have chosen. Or, it might be described as a church in which people see themselves as being "sent," rather than simply sending others. Either way, Guder argues that neither the structures nor the theology of the Western church is missional; rather Christendom's missions and models have been shaped by survival, acquiescence, and avoidance.[15]

However, there is a realm in which a missional understanding is prevalent, and that is the foreign mission field. In the realm of foreign mission an awareness that a culture is alien, even antagonistic to the church, is often a supposition. Little wonder it was missiologists such as McGavran, Wagner, and others who saw the Church Growth Movement as a reorientation of the church in the West along more missionary parameters.

Not surprising, young organic church growth thinkers are embracing Guder's seminal tome, for in it Guder has brought back the focus to the basics of church growth understanding: that God wants his lost people found, that unregenerate culture is antagonistic to such efforts, and therefore that every Christian has a crucial role to play in the missional process.

A Final Thought Before Our Journey Begins

One final word of advice, perhaps even caution. It is important to retain a judicious and analytical perspective toward practices and beliefs in the emerging organic church, as it is important to do so whenever Christians engage a culture. History is replete with examples of missional endeavors, including renewal or revival movements, that lost some of their initial focus and forte by aberrant theology or syncretism. But, just as revival movements such as the Reformation, the Wesleyan Revivals, the Great Awakening, the Holiness Movement, the Pentecostal/Azusa Street revivals, and the more recent Jesus Movement of the 1970s had heretical elements present at the fringes, the outcomes were that these movements helped reshape the church into more missional, and some would say more intended, manifestation of the Body of Christ. Though the reader should take the analysis and insights contained in the following pages with a grain of salt, I nonetheless sensed during my travels through the organic church that God may be reshaping the collective church's missional understanding once again.

Dr. Bob Whitesel
Indiana Wesleyan University
Associate Professor of Graduate Studies in Ministry
www.TheOrganicChurch.org
Creative Church Consulting Intl.
Winona Lake, IN 46590-0788
www.c3intl.org

THE PRELUDE

An Overview
of My Travels

How and Where Did My Journey Begin?

As a writer on generational issues for Abingdon Press, as well as a consultant and professor on church leadership and growth, I have had an insatiable appetite for investigating how the Holy Spirit is empowering Christians to share the good news. Subsequently, I have been investigating and analyzing what is happening in these emerging congregations with an eye toward helping both the emerging church as well as their parent churches understand how the Holy Spirit is leading his church to growth and health.

To gain this understanding, I commenced a journey over four years ago to participate in these churches, as well as to interview their attendees and leaders. In doing so, I have traveled from Sheffield, England, to Santa Monica, California; and from Edmonton, Alberta, to Baton Rouge, Louisiana.

Churches Were Chosen Not Because They Were Success Stories, but Because They Contained Transferable Lessons

From over forty churches, I have selected twelve for this present volume. Of these twelve churches, not all are success stories.

To focus merely on successful congregations would be a very boomer thing to do.[1] And thus, as the reader will discover, not all of these emerging churches have succeeded or survived. But all are examples through which I believe the Holy Spirit is weaving messages for the church's health, growth, and vibrancy.

Why a Journey?

In the chapter "Finale" that preceded this chapter, I described the so-called missional perspective that these young congregations embrace. They see themselves as missionaries, working amid a modern culture that is unsympathetic if not antagonistic to their message and efforts. I embrace this missional viewpoint as well and find their outlook not only more intentional than their parents' outlook, but also more wholistic and effective.

The organic church sees culture as something it must analyze and sift, judging certain elements and affirming others, for the transformation of the whole. Thus, because culture is so fluid, so too are their efforts. It is this elasticity that often leads them to describe the discipleship process as a journey. And as a journey, it may cross uncharted territory, encounter unforeseen surprises, take unexpected detours, but always be progressing, headed in some as of yet undisclosed or even undecided direction. This also means that since the time of my travels with these congregations, situations, venues, and names may have changed. Subsequently, I found it best to describe my encounter and convergence with them as a journey.

Finally, "journey" is a term that is helpful for this author, for it reminded me that though I traveled with them, I was never truly one of them. They are a generation born of the successes and failures of my generation, the boomers. And thus, they bear the weight of my generational missteps and dismissals. Yet, they were always more than willing to let me travel with them, and they truly seemed to enjoy my company. But the entire time there was an unspoken yet tacit impression that I was a guest.

Where Did "Postmodern" and "Emerging" Come From? And What Do They Mean?

Postmodernism began as an oxymoron fashioned by art critics to describe an avant-garde movement within the art world that emerged after 1914.[2] Earlier modernist artists such as Kandinsky, Klee, and Mondrian, on the one hand, had considered themselves mystics, breaking through the wall of appearances to a higher truth. Postmodern artists, on the other hand, believed they failed at this endeavor. In reaction, postmodern artists experimented with an organic and integrated mixture of media, varying genres and style. The postmodern artist drew from a plethora of artistic styles, often weaving them together to find a more engaging and authentic rendition. Thus, the steel cage design of Frank Lloyd Wright was wed with natural stone surfaces in his Kaufmann House and Taliesin studios. And sculptor Alexander Calder juxtaposed large metal wings in so-called mobiles that would drift softly on a natural breeze. This incorporation of the technological with the natural provided a new genre that could only be described as beyond the modernist project.

Postmodern is often preceded by the term "emerging" to describe an up-and-coming philosophical movement with four general characteristics: (1) It is wholistic, meaning it sees philosophy, religion, science, history, social theory, and the like as interrelated. (2) It believes you need to do more than talk about changing the world, you need to change it. Karl Marx stated, "Philosophers have only interpreted the world in various ways; the point is to change it."[3] (3) The scientific conception of facts is not trustworthy but is shaped by our interpretations. (4) And finally, vocabularies are shaped by our history. Thus, a term that has meaning to one person may need to be restated or contextualized to have meaning to another.

It is this later element that worries some critics of postmodern churches, because of a controversial axioms of postmodern writer/philosophers such as Richard Rorty who said, "Truth is what my peers will let me get away with." [4] As a result, such relativistic viewpoints alarmed moralistic boomers. Subsequently, the emerging church's association with postmodernity made the emerging church suspect. I reported in the preceding chapter that my research did not lead me to believe that they embraced the amoral aspects of postmodern philosophy, but rather they embrace a postmodern style and panache. As the *New York Times* stated, "Many emerging churches preach the same message as their sponsoring (evangelical) churches, but use different methods." [5]

The *New York Times* ignored artistic and philosophical underpinnings for the word "emerging," preferring to focus on the rising influence of this generation's efforts. "The label 'emerging church' refers to the emergence of a generation," the *New York Times* stated. Subsequently, in many of the online weblogs, chat rooms, as well in printed articles and books, Generation X has debated the appropriateness of "emerging" as a fair and useful descriptor of its efforts. Many note that emerging is tied to a point in time, and one day another movement may emerge and the emerging descriptor may need to be relinquished.

Regardless of its future, emerging church is the accepted designation at present. However, to overcome inconsistencies and limitations, as well as to describe more fully the usefulness of this generation's efforts, I will now explain why I believe that another, more organic descriptor better expresses their efforts.

Why "Organic" May Be Preferable to "Emerging"

A spate of names have been used to describe this thriving church culture. Appellations such as the "postmodern church," the "organic church," as well as the "emerging church" have abounded, with few resonating universally. The emerging church seems most broadly accepted, with researchers like Eddie Gibbs and Ryan Bolger preferring this appellation because it connotes a dynamic rather than a static entity.[6]

To add to the confusion over terminology, postmodernity customarily eschews labels because they cannot denote the flexible and fluid nature of a culture. But one of the above appellations does have a theological underpinning and potential fluidity that may make it a tolerable descriptor in a realm that shuns labels. Therefore, the most unobjectionable of these identifiers may be "organic," which has several rationales in its favor.

Antecedents and Validity in Theological, Social, and Political Disciplines

First, "organic" is a term that in theological and missional writings has consistently referred to a system of interrelated parts that make up a wholistic and healthy whole. Thus "organic" has generally described a church that is composed of a network of interdependent people who thrive in relative harmony as a living and growing entity.

In the Church Growth Movement, "organic church growth" is employed to describe this wholistic, growing, and healthy matrix of people and ministries. Charles Singletary asserts that organic church growth

> pertains to the infrastructure or cellular growth within churches. It consists of all sorts of sub-groups, small groups and networks so vital to the assimilation, nurture and mobilization of the membership. Organic growth involves the leadership and shepherding network of a church. Its health is normally a function of the number and quality of well-trained leaders or workers which are able to be mobilized in a local church context.[7]

This emphasis on a matrix of intimate discipleship groupings and missionally mobilized endeavors is a good descriptor of my observations of the organic church.

In addition, churches composed of a living network of ministries and leaders have been described by missional writer Alan Roxburgh as organic lay-led churches. Roxburgh recounts that the healthy leadership structures of the Free Churches of the Reformation were a "recovery of an organic, lay-lead church seeking to restore pre-Constantinian images of church and leadership."[8]

In a similar vein, Howard Snyder describes a healthy church as a "charismatic organism." By "charismatic," he suggests a church empowered by God, and by "organism," he emphasizes that all of its people are ministers.[9] This synergy between divine empowerment and collective participation is characteristic of the organic church.

In the social sciences, James F. Engel describes the "organic church model" as a growing and living network of people with five attributes: (1) one body, under one leadership, (2) equipped by God with supernatural giftings, (3) led by God through disciplined planning, (4) ministering to one another in community, and (5) ministering to the world.[10] Here again, a description of this wholistic and interrelated model closely parallels my observations of the organic church.

Political science employs the similar term "organic intellectual" to describe those who have the duty and skills to explain intellectual concepts to modern cultures. Although the author of this concept, Antonio Gramsci, used his understanding for self-centered ends, his term "organic intellectual" came to describe those who are skilled at helping a modern culture understand grand and pervasive concepts.[11] Gramsci believed such organic intellectuals were not just academicians, but also journalists, novelists, playwrights, authors, and media professionals. In addition, to accomplish their work, organic intellectuals study, experience, and analyze a culture, traveling along with it to better comprehend it. Finally, the organic intellectual contextualizes grand truths in terminology that a modern culture can understand, so as not to obliterate the modern culture. This idea of an organic intellectual that does not emasculate a culture, but sojourns along with it to translate grand understandings to it, mirrors the missional attitude of the organic church.

Antecedents and Validity in Scripture

"Organic" also connotes an interdependent and living organism, which Scripture employs as a metaphor for the church.

1 CORINTHIANS 12:12

The body is a unit, though it is made up of many parts; and though all its parts are many, they form one body. So it is with Christ.

1 CORINTHIANS 12:14

Now the body is not made up of one part but of many.

1 CORINTHIANS 12:20

As it is, there are many parts, but one body.

1 CORINTHIANS 12:27

Now you are the body of Christ, and each one of you is a part of it.

EPHESIANS 1:22-23

And God placed all things under his feet and appointed him to be head over everything for the church, which is his body, the fullness of him who fills everything in every way.

EPHESIANS 4:11-13

It was he who gave some to be apostles, some to be prophets, some to be evangelists, and some to be pastors and teachers, to prepare God's people for works of service, so that the body of Christ may be built up until we all reach unity in the faith and in the knowledge of the Son of God and become mature, attaining to the whole measure of the fullness of Christ.

COLOSSIANS 1:17-18

He is before all things, and in him all things hold together. And he is the head of the body, the church; he is the beginning and the firstborn from among the dead, so that in everything he might have the supremacy.

COLOSSIANS 1:24

Now I rejoice in what was suffered for you, and I fill up in my flesh what is still lacking in regard to Christ's afflictions, for the sake of his body, which is the church.

ROMANS 12:4-8

Just as each of us has one body with many members, and these members do not all have the same function, so in Christ we who are many form one body, and each member belongs to all the others. We have different gifts, according to the grace given us. If a man's gift is prophesying, let him use it in proportion to his faith. If it is serving, let him serve; if it is teaching, let him teach; if it is encouraging, let him encourage; if it is contributing to the needs of others, let him give generously; if it is leadership, let him govern diligently; if it is showing mercy, let him do it cheerfully.

Passages such as these remind us of the living, macrobiotic essence of the church, not as an organization, but as an organism.

Linguistic Validity

Finally, although the term "emerging" is fluid and dynamic, it also denotes a coming-out or an advent. As such, emerging will at some point become an ill-suited expression if the postmodern church wanes in flexibility and emergence. Although this author would hope that this would not be the case, church history is replete with examples of promising new experiments in discipleship, spirituality, and evangelism that become marginalized over time.[12] Thus the appellation "organic" connotes the living and networked characteristics of the organism, rather than its outward advent.

Therefore, because of missional, biblical, interdisciplinary, and linguistic legitimacy, the author will urge that organic be used as an equivalent descriptor for emerging, and thus the organic church will be preferred in this volume.[13]

Patterns of Organic Congregations

The Gospel and Our Culture Network, a network of Christian leaders from a wide array of churches and organizations, has been carrying on a lively discussion about the intersection of culture and Christ. Building upon foundational understandings of Richard Niebuhr,[14] Charles Kraft,[15] and Lesslie Newbigin,[16] this network of thinkers has produced a valuable set of written tools including The Gospel and Our Culture Newsletter and a spate of books. Summing up much of their conclusions, Craig Van Gelder sets forth in *Missional Church* what he calls the patterns of the "postmodern condition." Noted church growth researcher and writer Eddie Gibbs tendered an overview of these patterns in his book, *ChurchNext: Quantum Changes in How We Do Ministry.*

My current journey has allowed me to take Van Gelder and Gibb's observed patterns and apply them to case studies in these organic congregations. As such, I have found some to be incomplete, others to be increasingly obscure, but still more to be exact and accurate. Therefore, I have built upon my colleagues' inventory a more expansive and field-developed list. However, as the organic church grows and evolves throughout its spiritual journey, these demarcations will undoubtedly morph and adjust. And thus, the reader is encouraged to take this inventory as a baseline upon which to build one's own observations and analysis of the moving of the Holy Spirit among these organic congregations.

Figure 1. Postmodern Patterns and Organic Church Reactions

Van Gelder Patterns[17]	Gibbs Patterns[18]	Whitesel Additions	Organic Church *Reactions,* Whitesel[19]
Endless choices made available by technology			Varied times, styles, and locales of discipleship, worship, and spiritual experiences. Culture is studied and sifted, judging some aspects, affirming others, for the transformation of the whole.
Loss of shared experiences			Create community in small groups, and by clustering two to seven small groups.

Meaning conveyed as surfaces and images		Use of iconography, symbols, and liturgy to communicate Christian truths.
Transient relationships	Unpredictable world requiring a rapid response of "plan-do"	Membership is not required, only journey accompaniment. Change is inevitable; accept it and use it.
Plurality of approaches to sexual expression and experience		Sexual principles in the Bible are valid for Christians, but not obligatory for non-Christians until a conversionary experience.
Increasing two-tiered economy with many dead-end jobs		Low-cost, low-overhead church facilities, ministries, and salaries. Volunteerism is expected, even in executive roles. Solidarity with the poor and disenfranchised.
Personal spirituality without the necessity of organized religion	Decentralized networks	Meditation, personal journaling, personal Bible Study, and prayer disciplines are encouraged. Personal encounters with God are just as valid as corporate ones. Inter-church networks are based on personal relationships and commonalities, not on theology or history.

Random violence and clashes between cultures	Uncertainty in dealing with the present, and pessimism and paranoia in considering the future.		Christ is the only hope for wholeness and peace, but not for success or money. Churches must provide safe environments for women, children, and those emotionally and physically damaged.
Feelings of anger or resentment because somebody's left us with a mess	Same as above.		Boomer churches have got it wrong and are devoid (at least for the organic Christian) of spiritual mystery and encounter. Boomer churches have also disengaged themselves from the poor and disenfranchised.
	Change initiated at the periphery	Church structures change, and strategy is shaped by bottom-up forces and not top-down ones.	Organic churches stay connected to those they serve inside and outside of the church, adjusting strategy and ending ineffective ministries.[20] Those you serve dictate how you serve them. Understand a culture before you attempt to communicate with it.
		Search for transcendence in the mystical stories of the past.	Modern narratives are weak. Sermon illustrations that chart the preacher's weekly life

	pale in comparison to stories of Christian saints and sages.
Authenticity is preferred over excellence.	Quality in performance and execution can readily undercut authenticity and engagement. Keep it real, even if paltry and meager.
Ancient-future orientation	The church must be up-to-date as well as appreciative of traditions. Podcasts stream biblical sermons to attendees' iPods, while Byzantine imagery and disciplines create mystery and expectation in worship.
Experiment-ation leads to encounter.	Sleuthing the movements of the Holy Spirit leads to spiritual encounter, rather than structure. Ancient spiritual disciplines can be effective today.
Broad and frequent use of the arts is valid in evangelism and worship.	Wholistic approach to worship and evangelism means a variety of arts are valid during worship, as well as in social and evangelistic outreach. Musicians are only one category, among many artistic equals.

Ask-assertive environment.	It's okay to doubt and raise questions; everybody does. Spirituality is messy, not tidy. Questions are demarcations of the journey.

A Concise Hitchhiker's Guide

Time has never been a more powerful commodity than in today's fast-paced world of multitasking and multisensory encounter. Fuller Seminary professor Robert Banks points out that "we treat time as a non-finite resource, only to find it getting ever more scarce."[21] Thus, sometimes brevity and succinctness can be powerful learning tools.

Therefore, to aid in retention as well as to allow this book to be shared quickly and effectively with friends and colleagues, I have kept this book brief.

However, this brevity is calculated for one more reason. This journey is but a guidebook for other adventuresome souls who wish to track the workings and movement of the Holy Spirit. So, use this book as an abridged hitchhiker's guide that will hopefully inspire and encourage you to undertake your own travels among the organic church. As a result, your wonderment for God's power, workings, and even humor will be sustained and heightened.

A Roadmap to Our Tour

For continuity each chapter will follow a simple and parallel structure. The following is a short explanation for each of our travel segments.

First Encounters

Here I will set the scene by describing some notable memories from my first encounter with each congregation. In each instance, I will attempt to use interviews and first-person dialogue to allow the reader to delve into this organic culture and experience many of the same emotions and questions that inaugurated my journey.

Dashboard

A dashboard was originally a board used to stop mud from being dashed inside a vehicle. However today in our techno-savvy world, "dashboard" has evolved to mean a user interface that organizes and presents information in a way that is easy to grasp. In this book, in keeping with a travel theme as well as cyber verbiage, the term "dashboard" will be employed to present a short list of "fast facts" about the organic church under study.

A Fusion of Rhythms

In this section, I will describe the varying patterns I discovered on my journey. Though as the organic church mutates and evolves, these rhythms will change; a description of the mixtures I encountered can help readers grasp the mission and life as I experienced it in these congregations.

In addition, employing the musical term "rhythm" further describes how these patterns vary even within the fleeting occasion of my sojourn with each organic congregation. The rhythms tend to flow and ebb, sometimes more dominant, sometimes more inconsequential. And in much the same way that a melodious rhythm may return in and out of our consciousness, these rhythms give us a glimpse into the minds of the composers of these unique rhythms.

Shared Rhythms

In this segment, I will highlight rhythms that are frequently shared among organic congregations. I will also endeavor to highlight a collective rhythm in which each organic congregation is excelling.

The Rhythm of Place

In this segment, I will investigate unique patterns related to environments, atmospheres, and locales.

The Rhythm of Worship

Here I will investigate the unique expressions, ambiance, and articulations of adulation and praise. Not only will music be investigated, but a wholistic range of artistic expression such as dance, painting, sculpture, poetry, prose, film, theatre, video, and mixed-media.

I will also look at the flow and focus of worship, seeking to ascertain where it is headed, its historical antecedents, and why each element was deployed. Here we shall sift the organic church's motives, intentions, and orientations in worship.

The Rhythm of Discipleship and the Word

I shall attempt to lead the reader through the theological as well as practical underpinnings of each congregation's biblical content, transmission methods, how it connects people to the local church, and how the discipleship process unfolds.

Unique Rhythms

Paralleling the "Shared Rhythms" section, this segment will use the same three subsections: *The Rhythm of Place, The Rhythm of Worship,* and *The Rhythm of Discipleship and the Word.* Here, however, I will illuminate unique and distinctive patterns that can serve as the basis for transferable lessons.

An Interview with My Tour Guides

To ensure that this journey maintains a personal tone and does not digress into a stale travelogue, I have included a short interview with one or more key leaders. This interview will give the reader an opportunity to hear, as I did, insights from these innovative leaders in their own words.

What Every Church Can Learn

Lessons 1, 2, and 3

As I sojourned amid the organic church, I discovered its leaders had a voracious interest in the successes and missteps of other organic congregations. Eschewing a boomer predilection to stick with something that already works, the organic church seems to desire new ideas, creative methodologies, and innovative ideas that can be cross-pollinated.

Toward this end, I endeavored to end each chapter with three transferable skills or lessons that could lead to health and growth in both emerging and boomer churches.

For those wanting a QuickStart Guide to this book, consult these concluding lessons to glean the more transferable and germane insights from each chapter in a short three-lesson summary.

Those Who Made This Journey Possible

This journey would not have been possible without the gracious encouragement of my family for this protracted trek. My wife of thirty-one years, Rebecca, has been my best friend and encourager. And my four lovely and now-grown daughters, Breanna, Kelly, Corrie, and Ashley, have taught me much about how young people seek to indigenize worship to their youth culture.

My colleagues, our chancellor, Dr. Jim Barnes, and our president, Dr. Henry Smith, at Indiana Wesleyan University, where I serve as Associate Professor of Graduate Studies in Ministry, have been exceedingly flexible and gracious. Dr. Mark Smith, Dr. Jim Fuller, and Dr. David Wright, among others, have been effective sounding boards for my ruminations and viewpoints. In addition, the IWU students in the Master of Arts in Ministerial Leadership have been indispensable in critiquing my judgments and suggesting improvements. The office staff including Karen Clark and Joy Garman, along with Brandon Schaefer, our graduate assistant, have been helpful beyond expectations in codifying this endeavor.

My colleagues around the globe have likewise been indispensable to my understandings and theories. Dr. Eddie Gibbs, Dr. Pete Wagner, Dr. Kent Miller, Dr. Roger Finke, Dr. Kevin Dougherty, and Dr. George Hunter have been indispensable in their encouragement, as well as in their academic veracity. And my personal friends and colleagues Dr. Gary McIntosh, Dr. Ryan Bolger, Dr. Kent Hunter, Dr. Steve Wilkes, and Dr. Chip Arn have given the requisite personal friendship as well as professional insight to map out my journey.

Those sojourners with whom I have traveled alongside in the organic church are too numerous to name at this juncture. Instead they will be noted in each chapter as my trek unfolds. However, it was their collective love for our Lord Jesus as well as gracious support for me that made this journey a success.

And finally, my utmost indebtedness is to my Lord and Savior Jesus Christ, who took my stammering supplication of repentance and permitted me to work in his fields. I cannot state enough how his forgiveness and grace has helped me to undertake his Great Commission (Matthew 28:19-20) in the spirit of his Great Commandment (Matthew 22:37-40).

CHAPTER 1

St. Thomas' Church
Sheffield, England

And a believer, after all, is a lover; as a matter of fact, when it comes to enthusiasm, the most rapturous lover of all lovers is but a stripling compared with a believer.
— *Søren Kierkegaard, Danish philosopher*[1]

First Encounters

I was unprepared for my experience at St. Thomas', an Anglican church in Sheffield, England. Earlier that day I had perused their auditorium, a renovated warehouse that could hold barely one thousand people. And as a researcher and writer on church growth I knew that churches in Europe rarely grew over one thousand attendees, with even smaller gatherings in the Anglican Church and among younger generations.[2] Therefore I was astounded when arriving late for Sunday evening worship I found crowds of young people extending out the door. I estimated there were over seventeen hundred attendees, almost all under the age of thirty. I wondered what was happening, as I began a four-day exploration into one of Europe's fastest growing postmodern churches.

"Our story is really the story of a missional church with a clustered structure," explained former rector Mike Breen, who, sporting a plaid shirt, jeans, and closely cropped hair, looked nothing like my memory of an English rector. "By missional we mean a networked congregation where being 'sent' is stressed, rather than just sending others." He explained that writings by Darrell Guder and Eddie Gibbs[3] had led them to see a missional church as "an organism or tribe, unified by a mission to reach unchurched friends with utmost flexibility."

Dashboard

Church: Saint Thomas' Church (mother church) and The Philadelphia Church (daughter church)
Leaders: Mike Breen (former rector), Mick Woodhead (current rector), Paul Maconochie (pastor of Philadelphia campus), Anne MacLaurin (assistant pastor)
Location: Sheffield, England
Affiliations: Anglican Church of England, Baptist Union of Great Britain
Size: 1700+
Audience: Non-Christians, postmoderns, multiple generations, and diverse social classes throughout and around Sheffield, England
Websites: sttoms.net; tribalgeneration.com

A Fusion of Rhythms

Shared Rhythms

The Rhythm of Place

St. Thomas mirrors many organic congregations, meeting in unusual locations as availability and adaptability require. Originally headquartered within the stately stone walls of St. Thomas' Anglican Church, the church's growth drove them to lease Sheffield's largest disco: the Roxy. Within three years they had packed the Roxy, largely resembling an American mega-church. "We filled the Roxy but were really just like most mega-churches with brittleness and disconnection," recalled Paul Maconochie, a thirty-four-year-old former chemistry teacher and now one of the leaders tapped to replace Breen.

While one portion of the church grew in the downtown disco, the mother church also grew, choosing to continue worship services in the stately confines of St. Tom's. The church now resembled many organic churches with two distinct campuses, allowing them to provide diverse options in music, liturgy, and ministry.

The Rhythm of Worship

The two locations allowed experimentation in music as well as in liturgy. St. Tom's, now referred to as the mother church, hosted two Sunday worship services: a more traditional early service, followed by a modern service. The traditional service continued to draw traditional Anglicans from the neighborhood, while the modern option drew city residents who wanted updated worship that still retained traditional elements and atmospheres in keeping with the stately halls of St. Tom's.

The worship celebrations at the Roxy nightclub followed a more modern route. Today in a converted warehouse, this postmodern worship celebration embraces rhythmic music, testimonials from the crowd, prayer for salvation as well as for personal needs, and worship that is led by listening rather than by liturgy. When I attended, I noticed a leader on the platform holding a fist of archery arrows. He did not seem embarrassed, self-conscious, or even in the slightest way concerned about an explanation. It was not until later during his testimony did we learn that God had directed him to purchase arrows from the window of a small sports shop in Sheffield. Dutifully following what he perceived as God's leading, the leader encountered a distraught shopkeeper who responded joyfully to the encounter and was now in attendance at the celebration. More testimonials from the crowd followed, and while in many nonorganic churches, these testimonials might follow the format of praising God for some personal healing or need addressed; in this missional congregation, almost all of the testimonials were about connecting the good news to friends, relatives, and acquaintances. The tenor of the evening was one of

3

appreciation for God's Word, his power, and his desire to engage the Sheffield community.

The Rhythm of Discipleship and the Word

From its beginning to this day, St. Thomas' retains much of its Anglican heritage in its theology, its discipleship expectations, and its rites. And it parallels other organic churches by requiring a passage into leadership that crosses several well-defined demarcations. The Order of Mission (which they abbreviate to TOM) is the requisite and written strategy for those who wish to join the church. In TOM, attendees will find three levels of commitment.

The first stage of commitment is to become a "temporary," an introductory period that broadly parallels the novitiate in monasteries. During this time the temporary gains experience by participation in a lay-led ministry. This position is analogous to the new recruit in many nonorganic congregations; but in the organic church, it is seen not as end, but as a point of departure.

The second stage involves becoming a "permanent," which by its very name denotes a long-term commitment to the church and its mission. These will be the committed church leaders, which in nonorganic congregations are often the 20 percent that seem to do 80 percent of the work. However, at St. Tom's the expectation is that permanents will be managers, expected to direct and oversee ministry conducted by temporaries.

Finally, associates are individuals or churches who share St. Tom's missional perspective. This is St. Tom's way of defining those who are networked to it.

The church's missional perspective is clearly stated in TOM, in which under the heading "Why Establish a Missionary Order?" they declare: "We are living in missionary days. The Church in the West no longer finds itself situated in a pastoral context but a missionary one. Much of the Church, however, still operates as if it lived in the past—engaging, as a result, with fewer and fewer people every year." [4]

Inspired Rhythms

Inspired Rhythms of Place

Several years earlier, at the height of its popularity, St. Tom's had been informed that they would soon lose their lease to the Roxy, the only venue of such size in Sheffield. Although such a predicament is not unique, their reaction was. This news in nonorganic churches might cause consternation or at least annoyance, but the young leaders of St. Tom's saw a God-given opportunity to improvise with new forms of church structure.

While at the Roxy, small groups of seven to twelve people had been developed throughout the congregation. But the leaders had also experimented with clustering or combining two to seven small groups into what they called "missional communities" or simply "clusters."[5] Clusters ranged in size from twenty-five to eighty-five people and thus were flexible in time, location, and ministry. In addition, lay volunteers who were proved in small group scenarios led the clusters, expanding the lay shepherding base.

With a large venue unavailable, the leaders decided these weekly clusters would substitute for the all-church worship celebrations. Now, instead of gathering as a large impersonal congregation at the Roxy, the church met in seventeen-plus missional communities every weekend at seventeen-plus locations across the city. Since the average size of a cluster was twenty-five to eighty-five, St. Tom's now resembled a network of small churches meeting across Sheffield. They had created a city filled with small churches called clusters, which provided not only intimacy and familiarity, but also vision, focus, and direction.

However, the leaders also felt there were other ministry opportunities that required more person power than even a cluster of twenty-five to eighty-five people could muster. These opportunities would include expansive outreach to Sheffield's urban community, the popular dance club scene, the large University of Sheffield student body, fervent English sports enthusiasts, and a growing demographic of young professionals. To effectively impact and transform these English subcultures, something larger than a cluster of people would be necessary.

As a result they created "celebrations," gatherings of two to eight clusters and organized around social subcultures. Ranging in size from 125 to over 700 attendees, St. Tom's has over nine celebrations with names such as Connect (ministry to young adults), Encompass (ministry to specific neighborhoods), Mother Church (the original church in the Crookes area), Community Church at Crookes (an urban outreach based in Crookes), Expression (outreach to college students), Radiate (ministry to young adults in the workplace), and the Forge (inner-city ministry).

Celebrations meet for worship one Sunday a month, leaving the other three to four Sundays for the individual clusters to meet for worship and the Word. Celebrations include worship and teaching and give the smaller clusters a sense of a larger community. In addition, due to their size, celebrations foster community effectiveness and awareness. In addition, every Sunday evening, an optional worship gathering for all celebrations regularly attracts more than fifteen hundred young people and resulted in my first exposure to St. Tom's.

Inspired Rhythms of Discipleship and the Word

Another unique contribution is their use of symbols to help young people grasp the implications and requirements of discipleship. Similar to the icons of the Middle Ages designed to educate an illiterate populace, their use of symbols helps young adults bombarded by media-borne stimuli remember the essence of Christian discipleship.[6]

Recognizing we live in an "icon-driven" society, in which icons in Internet browsers or word processing programs convey a wealth of information, Rector Mike Breen sought out to convey the essentials of discipleship in an easy-to-remember series of geometric patterns. Called Lifeshapes©, below is a brief explanation of each.

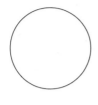

The Circle. The life of discipleship is like a circle: a process of lifelong learning in which God continually breaks in to cause us to reevaluate our progress. This may require us to go back and reexamine our basic commitment to Christ, our ministry, and where we have fundamentally changed from his original intentions.

The Semi-circle. This icon reminds us that there are rhythms of life, seasons with work and rest. Based on the Old and New Testament teachings of the Sabbath, healthy spiritual growth includes regular and seasonal respite.

The Triangle. Perhaps the most pervasively employed icon at St. Tom's, it conveys that the balanced Christian life requires three dimensions: (1) an upward relationship with God, (2) an inward relationship with one another, and (3) an outward relationship in evangelism and service to the world.

The Square. This reminds us that there are four phrases in the developing life of disciples: (1) call to follow, (2) a coming to terms with challenges, (3) delegation with oversight, and (4) the commission to go and make followers of Christ.[7]

The Pentagon. This reminds us of the five aspects of ministry in the body of Christ as set out in Ephesians 4. Here each disciple is reminded that God gives them opportunity to experience and flourish within five ministry roles.

The Toolbox. This icon underscores that God offers many other biblical gifts (1 Corinthians 12, Romans 12, and 1 Peter) and that these gifts are available to every believer as the Spirit directs and the need arrives.

These Lifeshapes© icons, while simple, are surprisingly effective in communicating the important elements of Christian discipleship to an increasingly visually driven and icon-based culture.

An Interview with My Tour Guides

Mike Breen (*former rector*)
Mick Woodhead (*rector*)
Paul Maconochie (*pastor of the Philadelphia campus*)
Bob Hopkins (*staff member*)

Clustering two to seven small groups into flexible, movable, and adaptable missional subcongregations has helped St. Tom's weather many storms. Today you have a sizable membership, with most under the age of forty.[8] Can you describe the role clustering small groups played in this growth?

Mick:[9] Clusters are adaptable in the times they meet, the places they meet, and the ministries they undertake. And clusters are small enough to share a common vision, yet large enough to do something about it. If a small group undertakes community service, some people won't show up and the group will be short-handed. Soon, the small group gets burned out. But clusters of small groups can staff and maintain community ministry longer because of their greater size.

Paul: And clusters are very effective in reaching new people. Small groups are often too intimate for new people to feel at home, and a big hall like the Roxy could be too impersonal. Therefore, when we knew we might lose our lease, we put our small groups into clusters and gave the clusters the responsibility of meeting once a week for worship and outreach.

Mike: The clusters are like a big extended family. It's like the movie *My Big Fat Greek Wedding*—you have your favorite extended relatives and even some eccentric ones. But you don't have to be chummy with anyone unless you want to. Young people crave this extended family experience because their families are disconnected.[10]

Can you give me examples of ministries that are suited to clusters?

Mick: One cluster hosts a drop-in café to feed homeless people, while others serve nursing homes by providing prayer, worship, and pastoral ministry. Many more clusters serve impoverished people. And some clusters reach out to preschoolers and their parents, providing childrearing advice, parenting courses, and baby-sitting services. All of these are long-term ministries to ensure they are effective, and the greater resources of clusters makes longevity possible. In all of these activities our goal is to be sent out and therefore connect people with similar interests to Jesus Christ.

It seems that clusters create flexibility in meeting places and times, opportunities to personalize outreach, and an indigenized environment that puts newcomers at ease. Have you seen other churches benefit from clustering their small groups?

Bob: Yes, one church is considering calling them 'mid-sized community groups' ... or MSCs for short.

Today, St. Tom's has evolved into two covenant-related congregations: an Anglican congregation at St. Tom's and a "daughter church" called the Philadelphia Church associated with the Baptist Union of Great Britain. Together they are composed of nine celebrations (groupings of clusters), with more than thirty-six clusters, uniting more than 170 small groups. And though St. Thomas/Philadelphia has navigated stormy waters, its ability to adapt and change while retaining its connectedness through clusters has led to what the leaders call "a networked church."

Do you have any parting thoughts?

Mike: Yes, it's a village really. A type of network composed of many celebrations, with even more clusters and many more small groups ... where everybody knows where they fit and what Christ sends them to do.

Four days of living among this adaptable and flexible congregation led me to agree.

What Every Church Can Learn

Lesson 1

Cluster small groups to maximize effectiveness. Church leaders will recognize that many missional tasks are better suited to the twenty-five to eighty-five people that a cluster of small groups can muster. Try combining small groups of similar interests and demographics for a specific task or opportunity. See if clustering groups doesn't allow you greater flexibility, longevity, and consistency in ministry.

Lesson 2

Use symbols and icons for retention and comprehension of important spiritual truths. Boomers have grown up in a society in which reading smaller and smaller books was the rule, not the exception. Clark Pinnock's influential apologetic *Set Forth Your Case: An Examination of Christianity's Credentials* was initially dismissed in 1967 as a serious Christian apologetic due to its small size (a four-by-six-inch paperback) and its short length (139 pages).[11] Yet for many boomers it became the requisite text to concisely refute early vestiges of postmodern culture. Today's youth are discovering in Breen's deceptively simple geometric icons an even more concise yet just as sophisticated explanation of Christian discipleship and authenticity.

Mike Breen's book *Lifeskills* describes these symbols in detail and explains how each connotes a biblical principle to a postmodern mind. Consider using these symbols and Breen's book, perhaps even indigenizing them to your local scenario.

Lesson 3

If your church averages over 125 adults each weekend, employ unity events to maintain cohesiveness. If church attendance is over 125, or if you host two worship expressions, you are probably becoming a congregation of two or more sub-congregations, whether you want to do this or not. Church researcher George Hunter noted that most congregations are really "a congregation of congregations."[12]

This, however, is not bad. On the onset, this scenario usually disheartens congregants because they fear drifting apart, united in name only. However, if the congregation is embracing a missional attitude, then having more venues and styles of worship services will allow the church to reach a larger segment of the community. Outreach thus trumps comfort.

St. Tom's exploited this missional flexibility when they launched a worship service outside of their stately stone walls and again later when the Roxy was lost as a venue. The result was that St. Tom's became a networked church of worshiping and missional clusters, meeting at different times, at different locales, with different styles to affect a larger segment of Sheffield.

However, there is also a natural polarization around these sub-congregations due to styles of worship, age-specific ministries, church campuses, geographic community, and so on. Thus, as subcongregations emerge, we must manage them in a way that maintains unity.

A key to preserving unity is regular, pan-congregational unity gatherings. Here are four guidelines:[13]

1. *Unity events can take many forms.* Typically we think of traditional all-church picnics and the like, but these must be carefully structured so that they are attractive to all subcongregations. And pursue creative options, including art events, ministry to disenfranchised people, seasonal worship expressions, travel, pan-congregational committees and teams, and so on.

2. *Planning and structure must be pan-congregational.* Success is predicated upon planning that involves representatives from all subcongregations. The goal should be an event structure and focus that is attractive to all subcongregations.

3. *Unity events must be regular.* Unity events can be designed to attract a large percentage of all subcongregations, or they can be planned to involve smaller segments of each. All church unity events should be scheduled at least four times a year, and smaller events should be encouraged three times a month.

4. *Make unity gatherings a fundamental part of your ministry.* To ensure that unity events develop into a core competency for your congregation, establish a standing committee/team that will oversee their frequency and veracity.

The need for unifying events is fulfilled at St. Tom's by both their once-a-month celebrations (gatherings of two to eight clusters) and their weekly Sunday evening gatherings. It is at this large Sunday evening expression with more than fifteen hundred in attendance that congregants get the sense of the true size of the church and are reminded that they are not marginalized, but part of something momentous in Sheffield.

CHAPTER 2

the sol café
Edmonton, Alberta, Canada

Worship leading is . . . "curating" (providing opportunities for engagement and free association).
— Sally Morgenthaler, worship consultant and author[1]

First Encounters

It looked like any other Internet café, with little indication a church gathering was about to take place. Feeling adrift, I made my way to the coffee bar. "I guess I'm the church greeter," began the barista. "I usually don't act so forward, but you looked lost." As a church growth consultant, I visit worship gatherings every weekend. But he was right, an unobtrusive beginning to this worship gathering had disoriented me. I didn't know the bewilderment was so obvious.

"We usually don't tell people a worship gathering is starting," continued the barista. "We just let them get comfortable, have a coffee, and engage in conversation. Then the worship unfolds slowly at an unhurried pace. We want to usher people into a spiritual encounter, we don't want to announce 'Hey, it's worship time: in or out!' "

I wondered out loud if people get offended once they discover a worship gathering is unfolding. "Rarely," replied the barista. "Most of the time people like the music, the unhurried atmosphere, patrons sharing their stories. It is a great way to do church, and it affects people who have never been to church. They are slowly led into a church experience. It's not dropped on them all at once."

True to the forecast, the evening progressed deliberately forward, but at a leisured pace. People laughed, talked, introduced themselves, and generally turned this Internet café into an extended family. Instrumental music was played at first, but soon some people were singing along. Over time more joined in, and even reticent attendees soon sang. At first the songs had a reflective timbre, but as the evening progressed so did the songs' Christian content, until finally I noticed many visitors were reflective and pensive. This unhurried evening would eventually culminate with a short interactive sermon.

"And we get even better attendance when its colder," reflected one of the leaders. "Edmonton is cold in the winter," he continued, "and the sol café provides a warm cup of coffee, good conversations, and time to reflect on life." Though usually frigid in January, Edmonton, Alberta, on this day resembled a spring afternoon. Yet good weather did not seem to deter a good turnout at the sol café.[2]

Dashboard

Church: the sol café [3]
Leaders: Debbie and Rob Toews (now employed as the director of a Christian retreat center), Anika and Steve Martin, Dave Wakulchyk (lay leaders)
Location: Whyte Avenue, an urban neighborhood in Edmonton, Alberta
Affiliation: Christian and Missionary Alliance of Canada
Size: 30-55
Audience: College/postmodern thinkers, metropolitan residents, urban artists, immigrant families, blue-collar families, people in their twenties to late-thirties
Website: www.thesolcafe.com

A Fusion of Rhythms

Shared Rhythms

The Rhythm of Place

"We wanted to create an atmosphere in which people could come and just sit around," reflected Rob Toews, the founding pastor. Jokingly he continued, "A pub was another option, but we didn't think the CMA[4] was ready for that."

The sol café had begun in the basement of a nearby Christian and Missionary Alliance church. However, the leaders felt that the catacombs of a local church would not adequately engage the postmodern thinkers in the neighborhood. "The church facility was a safe bet. It was available, and it wasn't costly," continued Rob. "But it also wasn't very effective."

They soon moved to a local Internet café, which eventually Rob and another couple purchased. During the week, they ran it as a business. Rob worked two to three shifts a week, selling coffee and conversing. Eddie Gibbs describes such risk-taking as a characteristic of the organic church, in which "uncertainty becomes an occasion for growth, not a cause of paralysis. It is a church prepared to take risks, which learns from its failures and mistakes."[5]

The Rhythm of Worship

The sol café's atmosphere was much of what I had come to expect, an organic fusion of low lighting, candles, caffeine, soft music, and comfortable chairs. The evening included what I had come to expect musically, a soft, almost plaintive style with simple instrumentation.

The Rhythm of Discipleship and the Word

Due perhaps as much to the caffeine-enriched environment as to their philosophy, attendees at the sol café asked questions and posited comments throughout the sermon. "A friend of mine and I were comparing notes about the failure of his postmodern worship gathering and the endurance of sol café," recalled Rob. "One reason is because at the sol café, interaction and asking questions are expected. In his fellowship, that wasn't the case." Routinely the organic church encourages didactic interaction, recognizing that young people want not to be lectured, but to be engaged.[6]

Sol café also sees itself as embracing a missional perspective: "That means we don't see reaching out as something we do; it's who we are. Evangelism isn't a program here," stated Rob. "It's part of the café DNA."

The sermon embraced an honest solidarity with the needy and poor in Edmonton, as well as an orthodox theology. "We feel called to be a church that is unapologetically Christian yet welcoming to people who are only generally interested in spiritual things," continued Rob. "We're a 'coffee stop' or 'information booth' along a spiritual highway. And that doesn't bother us. People will come through here, encounter Christ, and might wind up going to some other church. That's okay. It's about touching hundreds of lives every week with the love and message of Jesus."

Inspired Rhythms

Inspired Rhythms of Place

The use of an Internet café has allowed the sol café to daily engage its community. "One of our members wrote an introduction to the sol café," stated Rob. "He pointed out that it started as an idea . . . an idea just brewing in the back of our minds. The idea was this: If we wanted to get to know God better, we'd invite him over for coffee and have a good talk. After all, that's how we got to know all of our good friends. . . . And word gets around any time there's a good conversation and decent cup of joe to be had. We see the sol café as a 'gateway' or 'bridge' to a relationship with God."

Inspired Rhythms of Worship

Worship commenced in an unobtrusive and almost unnoticed manner. Instrumental music gave way to songs with which a few attendees might sing. Eventually, corporate singing would organically spill from the pattern. In fact, the Holy Spirit caught me unaware of his arrival, until I sensed myself drawn into reflection and contemplation. The sol café leaders allowed the Holy Spirit to begin his work first with my thoughts and then with my cares, by slowly setting the tone for God's work. Alan Roxburgh calls this an "openness to mystery and the understanding of God's own inscrutable work in our midst."[7]

The unannounced and unhurried nature of their worship also allows unchurched people time to acclimate to the workings of the Holy Spirit. This relaxed approach encouraged introspection and instruction as well as preparation. Finally, the slow swell and direction of the music appeared to lead even the most disinterested observer into a spiritual inventory.

Inspired Rhythms of Discipleship and the Word

The beginning of the sermon was uncomfortable, not for what was being said, but for what was going on. The barstool from which Matt Thompson delivered that night's sermon was positioned in front of the café's large glass windows, looking out upon the street. Thus, throughout the sermon, people passed behind Matt in a dynamic snapshot of daily life. Some passersby consumed by their daily tasks took little heed. Others, noticing a darkened room and a gathered group, peered inquisitively back at us. And a few, intrigued by the scenario, entered and joined our conclave. Although at first this backdrop of daily life was distracting, I soon appreciated how Matt's teachings about Jesus' love for the disenfranchised was deftly depicted out the café's large glass windows.

I discovered that this animated and living backdrop was intentional. Rob explained that one night they had extra musicians and had to set up in front of the large windows. Rob's former pastor was in attendance and remarked how this backdrop provided a window on their mission field. "We see it as a good thing," said Rob. "It keeps us focused on what we're about: to reach the people that walk the streets of Edmonton, to help them explore their relationship with God, and through this process to help them know what it means to follow him."

An Interview with My Tour Guide

Rob Toews (*founding pastor*)

The idea of purchasing a coffee shop as your hub of ministry was innovative and fiscally wise. Why didn't it financially thrive?

It worked, just not the way we expected. God's funny that way. The sol café continues to develop and do what we set out for it to do, both as a home church to a core group of "café regulars" as well as a "rest stop" or "information booth" for the wider community. But it was not able to sustain a paid pastor, and a concern over finances took our focus off of our mission.

We didn't realize that planting a church among people who don't have any church background takes more time and resources. We were working off of the typical model of a church plant, which usually is a church planted in a suburb. We didn't have a good model for going into the city, and thus we projected financial independence would happen faster than it did. But, the sol café in its current incarnation is small and intimate and still following God's call. The conversation continues.

What should have been done differently?

With an urban church plant you must commit to a longer process, with financial support lasting longer as well. Our denomination has a pretty standard support formula, and we just went with that. I think a better model would be to treat an urban church plant like an overseas mission. You really are reaching into an entirely different culture, with different sensitivities, a different worldview, even a different language. Thus, to reach the unchurched, you have to be prepared for lagging income. Base your support on whether you are bridging out to churched or unchurched people. The latter will require more time and resources.

Three Lessons to Consider

Lesson 1

Let worship emerge from your ambiance. Oftentimes a calculated and deliberate start to worship is not required. On the one hand, if you create an honest and authentic atmosphere of music, prayer, and personal introspection, then you can often linger and let the Holy Spirit guide you into an environment of adulation and praise. At this, the sol café excelled.

On the other hand, the boomer church is notorious for launching into worship with a gusto that mirrors the launch of a rock concert. But in the organic church, no such announcement or declaration seems necessary. Refreshingly, they allow the Holy Spirit to commence the evening, once a musically infused atmosphere of humbleness, introspection, and prayer has been fostered. Focus on establishing this authentic and unhurried connection, first among the musicians, then among attendees. Unveil rather than unleash.

Lesson 2

Use self-sustaining venues, realizing profitability may sustain the venue but probably not pastoral staff. Alternative venues such as cafes, used clothing stores, bookstores, tea bars, art venues, and music shops usually only sustain minimum-wage jobs. "The sol café was able to pay our baristas $7 an hour," recalled Rob. "But a pastor with a family is not going to be able to live on that." Although such venues are often self-sufficient, they may not be significantly profitable. Later in this book we will see how Church of the Apostles in Seattle uses a tea bar and art venue to support their church. However, again, revenue has only been sufficient to support facilities and not staff.

Lesson 3

It helps when a missional church can face its mission field. Facing the large front glass windows provided a missional backdrop for worship, interaction, and teaching at the sol café.

Although a backdrop of street-facing windows may be impractical for many organic congregations, live video images from a street outside or nearby can suffice. Elsewhere in this book I describe how The Bridge in Phoenix projected a grainy live video image behind the words of the songs, and the unfocused image created an inconspicuous but inventive backdrop. Churches interested in stressing their missional focus may wish to project unfocused images of nearby scenes of daily life behind the words to the songs. This can remind attendees of the daily activities and travails that go on concurrently with our worship celebrations. And such images can provide an engaging backdrop upon which God's love for humankind can be painted.

CHAPTER 3

Mars Hill
Grandville, Michigan

A community preserves a sense of unity despite differences and forces that seek to splinter it.
—*Stjepan Mestrovic, postemotional sociologist and author*[1]

First Encounters

When visiting organic communities, I have found it helpful to interview a person engaged in entry-level volunteer ministry. Such interactions often connect me with those who give insightful appraisals. I soon encountered Doug Luyk and explained to him the reason for my sojourn that morning with Mars Hill.

"This is a large church," I mused. "What's the key?" Although I was expecting to hear about the pastor's oratory skills or the church's popular music ministry, Doug quickly replied, "It's about small groups. Everyone needs to be in a small group. It's the purpose and power behind Mars Hill. Small groups are the 'church in the world,' not just the church on Sunday."

The remark was unexpected, but welcome. I wondered if Doug was a leader of a small group and thus might have a bias. After further conversation it became clear that Doug was simply a volunteer, who found small groups to be the glue that connected him to Mars Hill.

Dashboard

Church: Mars Hill

Leaders: Don Golden (lead pastor), Rob Bell, Jr. (teaching pastor), Joe Hays (student ministries pastor), Denise Van Eck (community life pastor)

Location: The former Grandvillage Mall in Grandville, Michigan

Affiliation: Nondenominational

Size: 10,000+ per week

Audience: People in their twenties to late-forties, middle to upper middle class, college/postmodern thinkers, multiple generations, dechurched and unchurched people

Website: www.mhbcmi.org

A Fusion of Rhythms

Shared Rhythms

The Rhythm of Place

At first encounter, Mars Hill feels like a boomer mega-church,[2] with a large auditorium filled three times on Sunday. The venue is a former mid-sized mall in the auditorium of a former anchor tenant. With little decoration, the iron beams and metal roof give the impression of a warehouse, which could easily be mistaken for the habitat of boomers. However, a closer inspection of Mars Hill's unassuming yet pervasive strategies reveals that this is not your father's mega-church.

The Rhythm of Worship

The worship setting and format share common elements with boomer churches, perhaps more so than they do with many organic churches. Due to the congregation's size, features of the organic church such as low lighting, interactive stations, comfortable chairs, and the like were missing. And the direct and concise format was similar to many boomer churches: twenty minutes of worship, an engaging sermon of forty minutes, followed by ten minutes of praise. Though the format was reminiscent of boomer congregations, the content was not, with a refreshingly modest and unpretentious spirit. This ability to create an unassuming ambiance amid a mega-sized congregation is a unique rhythm that will be discussed later in this chapter.

The worship music and its mode of presentation, however, paralleled other organic congregations. Worship songs by Matt Redman, Paul Oakley, and Delirious were given an edgy musical interpretation that fused together a spiritual rallying call with personal submissiveness and introspection.

The culmination of this atmosphere led—as it so often does in organic congregations—to an emphasis not on the music, musicians, execution, or even my enjoyment, but rather on the majesty and supremacy of our Lord Jesus Christ.

The Rhythm of Discipleship and the Word

The sermon embraced orthodox evangelical theology. And the sermon was delivered by a pastor in jeans and a simple shirt without a tie, making the speaker appear to be a college student rather than a shepherd of this sizable congregation. He did not shout or roar, but passionately engaged the audience with his viewpoint. Using extemporaneous humor, he allowed the audience to see him as one of them, albeit with a persuasive argument.[3]

The speaker also reminded the audience that "everyone here is a missionary, whether in a carpool or a cubical." Here again was a missional attitude, asserting that all attendees are missionaries, not just those who are sent to foreign locales.

In addition, the emphasis in all bulletins, church signage, and publications was not upon the pastors, but upon this missional direction of the congregants. Many nonorganic churches proudly feature the pastors' names on signage, bulletins, and so on, and as such may unconsciously perpetuate a philosophy that the pastor is the primary caregiver and minister. However, during my visit to Mars Hill, six large icons seemed to be the most pervasive signage. In fact, when I first entered the building, I stared at the large symbols above the entrance doors trying to ascertain if they were directional signage. Each icon was a variation on an arrow and was encompassed by a circle. Their simple and similar structure interested and engaged me, and soon I discovered they represent the essential nature of the congregation's missional thrust. The lack of the shepherds' names and the prominence of these icons gave this congregation a sense of purpose, rather than a sense of personality.

Inspired Rhythms

Inspired Rhythms of Place

Mars Hill meets in a former mid-sized shopping mall. Such community shopping malls, with only one or two anchor tenants and fifteen to twenty storefronts, are increasingly being closed, as bigger region-wide malls replace them. As a result, many communities are having difficulty finding suitable use for these facilities.

At Mars Hill, the sizeable hallways of an enclosed mall make good congregating points before and after worship. These wide corridors are also excellent conduits for human traffic flow, directing people to what was once the anchor tenant of the mall, and now anchors Mars Hill's worship gatherings.

On my way to the auditorium, I passed many former storefronts that now provided convenient and aesthetically pleasing locations for children's ministry. Through these windows a visitor can take in the life and vibrancy of the children's ministries. Making the children's ministry accessible and visible is something that should be incorporated in more church designs, for as I walked toward the auditorium I was exposed to the life, energy, and intergenerational community of this congregation.

Inspired Rhythms of Worship

The auditorium was bereft of decoration. However, the location and ambiance of the stage was unique. Although some churches might locate the stage at one end of the auditorium, Mars Hill places it in the middle.[4] With seating on four sides, the theatre-in-the-round effect ensures all seating is nearer to the speaker. This engages the audience members and allows a large church to retain some of its intimacy.

Initially I wondered if the worship team would be hampered by this encircling milieu. However, they overcame this by arranging musicians and singers at the four sides of the stage, but facing inward. This required all worship leaders to look at one another, and then beyond to the audience across the room. This not only allowed musical synchronization, but also kept the worship team from being the focal point, by placing them across the stage from the audience. This unifying yet unpretentious arrangement permitted the music and the worship it generated, and not the musicians, to be the focus.

Inspired Rhythms of Discipleship and the Word

There are numerous exceptional rhythms at Mars Hill, but two require closer inspection. One is the use of iconography, and the other is the unrelenting expectation that all attendees will participate in a small groups.

Iconography

Mars Hill uses six innovative icons to remind and enthuse congregants with their biblical mission. Large banners with these icons—called DIRECTIONS©—adorned the doors and hallways, reminding people of the essential elements of their missional lifestyle. Figure 2 illustrates these icons, followed by a short overview of their meaning.[5]

Figure 2. DIRECTIONS©

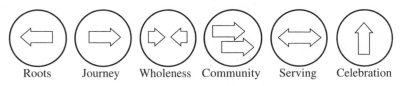

| Roots | Journey | Wholeness | Community | Serving | Celebration |

Roots: Mars Hill Church sees themselves amid a long line of generations participating in an ongoing conversation between God and people. Thus, the Bible contains God-inspired voices of those who have come before, sharing their poetry, narratives, stories, "and letters of response and relationship with each other and the living God."[6] Such a perspective allows the church to know where it is going because it knows where it has been. Richard Niebuhr, describing the tension between Christ and culture, labeled this the conversionist perspective, stating, "For the conversionist, history is the story of God's mighty deeds and of man's responses to them. He lives somewhat less 'between the times' and somewhat more in the divine 'Now' than do his brother Christians."[7]

Journey: This stresses that the church must discover innovative ways to communicate and live out Jesus' teachings. And, "because we see this as a journey, change is assumed, innovation is expected, and rebirth is welcomed."[8]

Wholeness: Jesus' message is holistic as is our response; meaning when we offer our mind, body, and soul to him, he repairs the damage of our failures, worries, and shattered lives.

Community: Bearing one another's burdens, sharing possessions, praying, the confessing of sins, suffering together, and celebrating collectively direct us toward an authentic and altruistic community.

Serving: The church is called "to relieve suffering and fight injustice, living out the transforming message of the resurrected Jesus. ... We were created to live for something larger than ourselves."[9]

Celebration: The world God originally created is good, with people created in his image. Thus "no amount of darkness can erase that divine imprint." Subsequently God's fingerprints are everywhere, allowing Mars Hill to celebrate his benevolence, munificence, and goodwill toward his creation.[10] This again parallels Niebuhr, who argues that "man's good nature has become corrupted; it is not bad, as something that ought not to exist, but warped, twisted, and misdirected."[11]

Small Groups

Though Mars Hill has been called an organic church, it has also grown to the size of a mega-church. And though some believe mega-church and organic to be mutually exclusive categories, the proliferation of small groups, or "house churches," has allowed Mars Hill to retain much of the intimacy characteristic of the organic church.

Attendees fill out a House Church Request Form to discover which house church is right for them. Then one of four full-time regional pastors guides each participant into the proper environ.

A grassroots rather than a top-down orientation is maintained by allowing individual house churches to determine their size, timing, location, ministry, content, and focus. Kindra Voorhies, the administrative assistant in the Community Life Ministries, summarizes, "Our main hope is that people will take house churches beyond the idea of a Bible study and will do life together: outside the four walls of the church, living out the call of Christ, living as Christ-like as possible, serving neighbors together, reading scripture, eating together, listening, sharing, and living in *true* community together."

Researcher Win Arn noted that attendees of large churches "need to form many responsible groups both for their own growth and for the growth of the church. They need to relate. They need to identify. They need really to know one another so members are not lost in the bigness of it all." [12] This describes well the spirit of Mars Hill.

An Interview with My Tour Guides

Denise Van Eck (*community life pastor*)
and Kindra Voorhies (*community life administrator*)

How is your house church network structured?
Kindra: We divided West Michigan into four geographic regions, with a full-time pastor serving each. Within each region, clusters of eight to ten house churches are grouped into "neighborhoods." Leadership development, training, and much of our local missional expression happens at the neighborhood level. And within this structure, house church pastors serve as guides.

What do you mean they are guides?
Kindra: House church pastors are similar to whitewater rafting guides. A guide doesn't do all the paddling to get the raft down

the river; everyone in the boat paddles. The guide is there to steer them down the right path.

Is there a proscribed time, focus, or frequency for house churches?

Denise: A lot of people ask, how often should house churches meet? Again, there is no formula for this. A house church "meeting" could be a set time to study and pray, or it could be a baseball game or school play. It could be painting someone's house or taking in a movie together. The healthiest communities find a rhythm that incorporates the realities of our complicated lives with the commitment to being true followers of Jesus.

Kindra: It is really up to the house church leader and the house church to determine what the group will focus on, who will be a part of it, and how many members is the right number.

Any parting thoughts?

Denise: A house church is not utopia—in fact, house churches tend to be a bit messy. No one has yet figured out how to do it all perfectly. The beauty of a house church is that as we do the journey together, we find the community that we long for, even when it's not perfect.

Three Lessons to Consider

Lesson 1

Encourage participation in small groups to retain intimacy, accountability, and mission. Researchers such as Peter Wagner, Eddie Gibbs, and Lyle Schaller have demonstrated that small group settings are the primary environments in which discipleship and healthy church relationships develop.[13] These groups are often described as three to twelve people[14] in an environment that is "people centered...characterized by intimacy and interpersonal engagement."[15] They usually meet on a semi-regular basis, out of which accountability, discipleship, and mission arise.[16]

Retaining familiarity and interdependence as a church grows is a well-documented problem. English researcher Peter Brierley analyzed English church attendance in the 1990s and discovered that large churches increasingly have difficulty maintaining growth as they increase in size.[17] Analyzing this data, Oxford professor of historical theology Alister McGrath ascribed the problem to "having reached a critical mass, larger churches began to lose the sense of 'belonging' that is such an important theme in postmodern culture."[18]

At Mars Hill, "house churches" address this potential disconnect as the church's weekly attendance hovers around ten thousand. House churches are a core competency at Mars Hill,[19] providing smaller, more intimate and accountable family infrastructures. Rodney Clapp argues that this aligns better with the New Testament, which did not intend the church to be an institution, but a family in which "those who do the will of the Father (who, in other words, live under the reign of God) are now brothers and sisters." [20] Small groups help Mars Hill retain this sense of kinship as the congregation grows and as biological families scatter.

Conversations in the mall corridors of Mars Hill also revealed that congregants see the house church network as a fundamental, if not essential, part of their outreach. "Small groups are the church in the world," stated Doug Luyk, with more passion than I anticipated, "not the church on Sunday." Missiologist Donald McGavran described such an attitude as "outward-looking." [21]

However, for small groups to proliferate in a growing church, they must be created organically rather than artificially.[22] This means that we must not simply assign people to a group based upon age or location and expect them to thrive in this artificial environment. Because camaraderie and affinity are created by more factors that just proximity in locale or age, an organically designed small group system delves into many commonalities before assigning people into small groups. Mars Hill advocates this organic approach to small groups through their Community Life Department, which uses questionnaires and interviews to connect people with an appropriate house church.

Thus, as a church grows, so, too, must its infrastructure of organically created small groups in which intimacy, connectedness, discipleship, and mission are fostered. If growth in this network is not directly proportional to your growth in size, brittleness, factions, loss of intimacy, and group exit will result.[23]

Lesson 2

If feasible, look for underused or vacant mid-sized malls as potential church facilities. For over half a century, shopping malls have been designed to create community, leisureliness, and engagement for shoppers. Now, the same interpersonal dynamics can be attained when churches appropriate such facilities. Architects of malls are skilled at recreating the leisurely pace of Main Street America, with fountains, benches, foliage, and locales for rest, respite, and interaction.

In addition, the traffic flow at Mars Hill was the best of any church I have visited in years, including many mega-churches with new facilities designed by noted architects. The large mall corridors meandered efficiently but purposely toward the former anchor tenant location and current worship gathering space.

Finally, an ability to transform the mall storefronts into children's ministry centers, youth venues, cafés, bookstores, and the like means you can capitalize on a professional architect's skill in building community and repose as well as engagement.

Lesson 3

Use technologically up-to-date tools such as short DVDs to communicate truth. Mars Hill uses a series of twelve-minute short films on DVD to communicate the Bible's teaching to young people. The films are an artistically rendered fusion of images, commentary, storytelling, and music. Plus, with the rise of user-friendly and low-cost computerized film editing tools, such mini-films can be readily crafted by church artisans eager to communicate truths to a postmodern mind more acquainted with video clips, sound bites, and movies than with the Bible or theological commentary.

CHAPTER 4

The Bridge
Phoenix, Tempe,
and Scottsdale, Arizona

Every human society is like a town on one side of a river over
which at convenient places bridges have been built.
—*Donald R. McGavran, missiologist and*
founder of the Church Growth Movement[1]

First Encounters

It was a precarious perch. The fire escape was several floors above the parking lot, and its rickety character did not instill a sense of confidence. But this was the location I was allotted for an interview with the pastor of an organic church that is building a unique bridge to both college students and the poor in Phoenix, Arizona.

"Two things get me excited," stated Aaron Norwood, "My heart beats for college students, and my heart beats for the poor." A longish goatee without the requisite mustache seems to almost fall from his chin. Short cropped hair and this goatee make Aaron look older and rougher than his thirty-one years.

Another surprise was the location, for though this was a Southern Baptist church, they met Sunday evenings in the event hall above a college bar in Tempe, Arizona. In fact, to find the worship service I had either to negotiate the rickety fire escape or to pass through the bar. Despite its arresting look, I chose the fire escape and at its crest met Aaron.

This Southern Baptist congregation, however, is not unlike other Southern Baptist congregations in message or goals. "We're here to lead college-aged people to Christ, that's for sure," continued Aaron. "But we are also here to help poor and hurting people in Phoenix. Reaching success-bound college students and reaching poverty-trapped Phoenix residents shouldn't be opposites. They should be part of every church's mission."

He was right. In the organic church I have consistently witnessed a passion to reach out to the disenfranchised, as well as to the upwardly mobile. The Bridge in Phoenix, Arizona, is a fitting example of fulfilling both the Great Commission and the Great Commandment.

Dashboard

Church: The Bridge
Leaders: Aaron Norwood (pastor), Blake Murchison (worship leader)
Location: Three worship and ministry locations: Phoenix, Tempe, and Scottsdale, Arizona
Affiliations: Southern Baptist Convention
Size: 155+
Audience: Students, young professionals, postmoderns, twentysomethings, seekers, homeless and urban poor
Websites: thebridgewebsite.com; riovistacenter.com

A Fusion of Rhythms

Shared Rhythms

The Rhythm of Place

Conducting ministry in locales that are both familiar and accessible, regardless of notoriety, is a common trait in the organic church. These young leaders see the locale as a strategic element of their mission.

Not surprising, for two and a half years the Bridge had gathered to worship in Arizona's leading nightclub, Club Freedom. "We'll never forget the musty stench in the air, the lack of air conditioning (or extreme opposite), and the hurry-up tear-down routine—

often tearing down our equipment just hours before one of the world's top DJs performed," mused Aaron. More recently, a college bar in Tempe and a nightclub in Scottsdale provided weekly venues for connecting with young adults. "It makes it easy for people to find us," stated Aaron. "And it lets people from the bar find their way to church." These popular locations and familiar spaces proved the Bridge an effectual "passage" to the youth culture.

Donald R. McGavran, missiologist and father of church growth theology,[2] crafted the imagery of missionary work as "building a bridge" to another culture: "Every human society is like a town on one side of a river over which at convenient places bridges have been built. Citizens can cross the river at other places, but it is much easier to go across the bridges. . . . As congregations administer for church growth, they ought to discover and use these bridges to the unreached. Good stewards of the grace of God should remember the bridges and stream across them. 'Find the bridges and use them' is excellent strategy for all who are impelled by the Holy Spirit to share the Good News." [3] The leadership of the Bridge embraced this strategic initiative.

The Rhythm of Worship

Though the locale was unconventional, the worship was consistent with many of my other experiences in the organic church. The worship was authentic, honest, and frank. Interactive stations ringed the room, allowing attendees to roam to various locations and participate in interactive activities during the worship segment. One station included eight tablets, each with a scripture that pertained to that night's message. Congregants were encouraged to write their reflections underneath and to read the reflections of others. A sort of communal journaling, this allowed attendees to get a sense of how the Holy Spirit was moving among attendees that night.

The stage setting also lent an air of authenticity, as well as a rebuff to any vestige of professionalism or performance. The screen upon which the lyrics were projected was a simple but skewed bedsheet. I mused about how battles had been waged in boomer churches over hanging an expensive video screen, and now boomer heirs casually drape a bedsheet almost with audacious glee. And though the words were legible, behind them was a grainy image of people milling about and working on some unintelligible project. I soon realized this was live video from a camera focused on one of the interactive stations. The image, grainy and coarse, did not distract due to the blurring of details. But it did add to the unspoken sense that worship was more than just singing, but was also an engagement of one's entire body, mind, and soul.

The Rhythm of Discipleship and the Word

Though the locale and ambiance were not what one might expect in a Southern Baptist church, the message and theology were. The sermon that evening was an especially poignant lesson on trusting God even when you do not see him. With copious doses of scripture and Christian thinker St. Augustine, Aaron reminded the audience that neither relativistic academicians nor personal loneliness meant that God was not close at hand. He quoted Augustine, "Faith is to believe what we do not see, and the reward of this faith is to see what we believe."

After an engaging sermon, Aaron drew everyone's attention to a commitment card. Reminding them that following Christ is neither effortless nor comfortable, he invited attendees who wished to do so to sign the "Commitment Covenant" form. This sermon and celebration above a college bar had led to a point of decision and commitment, not unlike what was happening that night in other Southern Baptist churches across North America.

Inspired Rhythms

Inspired Rhythms of Discipleship and the Word

A noteworthy rhythm was how the Bridge balanced both the evangelistic and the culture mandates. In the first chapter, I explained how the evangelistic mandate, on the one hand, is Christ's commission, exemplified in Matthew 29:18-20, to make disciples or "active learners" by going, baptizing, and teaching about Jesus.[4]

The cultural mandate, on the other hand, complements and completes the evangelistic mandate by requiring Christian energies be directed to meet the physical, emotional, and safety needs of God's creation. Peter Wagner declared,

> The cultural mandate has never been rescinded. . . . Every Christian and every church must contribute in some way to the effective fulfillment of the cultural mandate. It is not enough to think and theologize about it. It takes doing. It is not enough even to pray about it. It takes energy and involvement.[5]

Unfortunately, twenty-plus years of church growth consulting has led me to believe that most churches err on the side of one mandate or the other. And within many boomer churches, the unbalance is customarily in favor of the evangelistic mandate. Such bias can erode our validity and legitimacy with compassionate nonbelievers. And as such, our ability to dialogue with socially active friends is damaged, stained by a perceived nonaltruistic bent on the behalf of the church.

No such bias seems to pervade the Bridge. While many growing churches of educated young people might decide to purchase facilities in the suburbs, when growth allowed the Bridge to purchase a building, they purchased an inner-city clothing and food distribution center. The Bridge leaders saw this as an opportunity to put their offices and ministry in the midst of the people they served. I described in an earlier book how a common characteristic among growing churches is for church leaders to distance themselves from those they serve.[6] Typically the comfort and convenience of a growing staff garners priority, justifying moving out of urban areas as affluence and success follow growth.

Such estrangement has not ensnared the Bridge. True to their name, they remain a bridge to young adults and to the inner city. The food and clothing center, known as Rio Vista, is not only the home of their offices, but also the center of their Sunday worship celebrations where they host their core Sunday event called "the Sunday Brunch." This is a worship celebration followed by a full meal for the many people in the area who are poor or homeless.

Though the church still holds three other worship services at other venues, they still focus on the Sunday Brunch as "the service." This focus upon a Sunday brunch of spiritual and physical nutrition reminds congregants of the duality of their mission.

An Interview with My Tour Guide

Aaron Norwood (*pastor*)

How did this focus on the needy come about?
We began to focus on the homeless and urban poor because this is a command that runs all through Scripture. Micah 6:8 is one of our theme verses, "And what does the LORD require of you? To act justly and to love mercy and to walk humbly with your God."

Describe a typical Sunday Brunch.
The Sunday Brunch is our worship gathering and outreach ministry at Rio Vista, a food and clothing distribution center we purchased.

9:15 AM. We start with classes for youth and adults; a typical Sunday school model. We call them community groups, and some meet in homes and restaurants during the week. The importance of small groups comes from my Southern Baptist philosophy. And in an urban area, Sunday school–style groups work better than hosting them in homes during the week.

10:17 AM. Sunday Brunch starts with our band playing covers of U2, David Crowder, Switchfoot, and other musical groups. While the music is playing, people go through a full-service cafeteria line. No one really sings during this time; people are just talking and eating. People get seconds, and we hold a children's class during this time called Mini-Bridge.

10:47 AM (approximately). I begin speaking for fifteen minutes while people are finishing. I end with a focused prayer time. This is sort of an invitation, but it allows people to apply the sermon to their need and then respond in prayer. I suggest prayer topics for them at different levels and give everyone a chance to respond however they require.

11:00–11:10 AM. This is followed by worship during which everyone joins in. It is a fitting conclusion to the ministry of service and the Word.

11:10 AM–12:30 PM. People spend the rest of the time fellowshiping, talking, and getting to know one another. The band plays on, and it's a relaxed time. There is no ending point; people just leave when they are done.

A recap would be that the Sunday Brunch can be loud and chaotic in the beginning, but in the middle it simmers down and then bubbles back up at the end.

You describe the Sunday Brunch as "the service." Why?
We want people from the nightclubs to serve the urban people, and this is where "the service" takes place. We talk about this all the time. We let people tell their stories about how God is using them to help others.

How do you keep four worship gatherings at three locations unified?
Regularly on Sunday afternoons we bring together everyone from all the worship gatherings at Rio Vista. We call it "Reconnect." We have a meal, baptisms, and communion, and then we focus on testimonies. Reconnect is a unity gathering that gets everyone from the three different venues together and on the same mission.

Any parting words?
Solidarity with the poor and homeless has to start with the leaders. The leaders have to be volunteering and interacting with them if they are going to keep serving the poor. When the leaders think they are too busy for this, a warning should pop up.

Three Lessons to Consider

Lesson 1

Balance both the cultural and the evangelistic mandates. To balance these mandates, it is helpful to begin with an understanding of both mandates' influence upon the decision-making process. And this influence can be visualized by using the Engel Scale, a visual representation of the spiritual decision process.

Early on in the spiritual decision process (represented by the negative numbers on the Engel Scale), the influence and veracity of the cultural mandate dominates. But later in the process (toward the positive end), the evangelistic mandate increases in vigor. It is important to understand that at the same time, but also in varying degrees, both of these mandates influence and affect the decision-making process. I have illustrated in figure 3 the symbiotic relationship between the Engel Scale and the poignancy of each mandate.[7]

Figure 3. The Relationship Between:

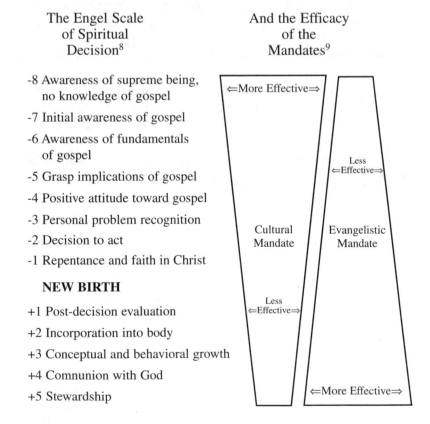

The Engel Scale
of Spiritual
Decision[8]

And the Efficacy
of the
Mandates[9]

-8 Awareness of supreme being, no knowledge of gospel

⟸More Effective⟹

-7 Initial awareness of gospel

-6 Awareness of fundamentals of gospel

Less ⟸Effective⟹

-5 Grasp implications of gospel

-4 Positive attitude toward gospel

-3 Personal problem recognition

Cultural Mandate

Evangelistic Mandate

-2 Decision to act

-1 Repentance and faith in Christ

NEW BIRTH

Less ⟸Effective⟹

+1 Post-decision evaluation

+2 Incorporation into body

+3 Conceptual and behavioral growth

+4 Comnunion with God

+5 Stewardship

⟸More Effective⟹

The Engel scale is a visual reminder that a spiritual decision is a dynamic process-driven model and not just a static conversionary point. Eddie Gibbs cautioned that "within evangelical tradition there has been an undue emphasis on the conversion *event,* to the neglect of an understanding of conversion as a lifelong *process.*"[10] Thus, visualizing the flexible relationship between the Engle Scale and the dual mandates instills a progressive and missional perspective that can be maintained against the more fêted conversionary event. The Bridge recognizes and embraces this balance.

Lesson 2

The cultural mandate must be carefully studied and replicated, not only because of its strategic importance, but also because evangelicals lack proficiency. Assessing one hundred years of evangelical activity, historian Sherwood Wirt lamented, "The social impress of evangelical Christianity between 1860 and 1960, apart from its missionary outreach, must be judged a failure."[11] My work training pastors in the College of Graduate Studies at Indiana Wesleyan University as well as my consultancy work have led me to believe little has changed since Wirt's disquieting assessment.

A balance between the cultural and evangelistic mandates has been described by the Christian Response to Evangelism and Social Responsibility, a consultation convened by the Lausanne Committee for World Evangelization, as "the relationship between two wings on a bird or two oars in a boat...being inseparable."[12] The fundamental interdependence between these dual mandates is well served by this imagery. Yet, due to the evangelical church's failure adequately and pervasively to embrace both, might we say the evangelical church has been grounded or, even worse, rowing in circles?

This need for social action and evangelistic effort to take wing is what the organic church is observing and seeking to address. But models are few, and social capital has been squandered by poor performance. Again, Sherwood Wirt lamented,

When the evangelical rises from his knees with a vision of Christ's compassion for the world, however, he faces a problem. Not only is he handicapped by inexperience and by an unsatisfactory immediate past; he is also hobbled by the world's suspicion, which is not entirely based on false suppositions.[13]

Thus, today's congregations must investigate and replicate examples of compassion as exemplified in the organic church, Roman Catholicism, other Christian denominations, as well as religious and secular service agencies.[14] The evangelical church cannot simply concentrate on the evangelistic mandate and still retain its integrity with the world.

Lesson 3

Concerted effort will be required to keep the two mandates in balance, even among the organic church. Unfortunately, to date the church has not been broadly successful in balancing the cultural and evangelical mandates. In 1968, while lamenting the lack of social conscience in the church, Wirt gleefully described a growing movement among young evangelicals to address this inadequacy. Optimistic, Wirt wrote,

What the evangelical of the sixties wants to do is to return the church to its historical Biblical position of concern for society. The thousand missionary and church leaders who signed the "Wheaton Declaration of 1966" confess, "We have sinned grievously. We are guilty of an unscriptural separation from the world that too often keeps us from honestly facing and coping with its concerns. We have failed to apply scriptural principles to such problems as racism, war, population explosion, poverty, family disintegration, social revolution and communism."[15]

Such lofty affirmations should be lauded. But, although many who signed this confessional became the evangelical leaders of the 1970s and of today, Wirt's optimism did not come to fruition. Herein is a lesson for the organic church as well as for the boomer church, that despite intentions and initial success, balancing the cultural and evangelistic mandates is a precise and arduous endeavor.

Thus, regularly evaluate your programming to see if an inordinate proportion is directed toward the evangelistic process. Then ask yourself, are there areas that you need to develop and expand so that you can have a wholistic and balanced outreach to our world in both the evangelistic mandate and the cultural one? Not to do so not only drives many young Christians from our churches, but also may undermine our authenticity with those we seek to reach.

CHAPTER 5

Vintage Faith
Santa Cruz, California

A postmodern artist or writer is in the position of a philosopher; the text he writes, the work he produces are not in principle governed by preestablished rules.
—Jean-Francois Lyotard, French philosopher who introduced the term postmodernism into philosophical discussion[1]

First Encounters

The campus of Santa Cruz Bible Church seemed the antithesis of an organic church setting. Neatly trimmed hedges embraced meandering sidewalks amid beautiful window-laden buildings. Vintage Faith Church had grown out of the college ministry of this congregation and currently worshiped in this boomer church's multipurpose worship gymnasium.[2] I wondered how Vintage Faith could create in this utilitarian space an atmosphere engendering the mystery and wonder of God so preferred in organic milieus.

The answer arrived as I entered. Dark curtains surrounded me on all sides. Vintage Faith's simple stage was off center and thrust into the audience. Three large media screens were placed along a long wall, and on the ends of the auditorium were two "mood walls" on which colorful yet muted images of young people lifting their hands in worship imbued this room with a 270-degree sense of expectation. A six-foot metal cross graced the center of the stage, flanked by two candles and a large oil painting depicting a stylized cross. And though this was a bright sunny day, the low lighting, visual images, curtaining, candles, and encompassing artwork transformed a contemporary gymnasium into a peaceful, subdued, and sacred space.[3]

Dashboard

Church: Vintage Faith Church
Leaders: Dan Kimball (pastor), Josh Fox (pastor of musical worship), Robert Namba (pastor of spiritual formation), Hannah Mello (director of worship arts), Kristin Culman (communications and hospitality)
Location: Santa Cruz, California
Affiliation: Nondenominational, though assistance is provided by Santa Cruz Bible Church
Size: 375-450. "That's an estimate," states Dan Kimball. "We don't count people, we count leaders."
Audience: Multiple generations, college students, university personnel and faculty, artists, and pre-Christians—people who are spiritually sensitive
Website: www.vintagechurch.org

A Fusion of Rhythms

Shared Rhythms

The Rhythm of Worship

Worship at Vintage Faith is a fusion of original and current worship music, along with some surprising but effective reinterpretations of classic praise songs. In the latter category was an improvisational rendition of "We Are One in the Spirit," which was created while attendees visited interactive worship stations.

The format followed many organic church configurations. However, to an initial twenty minutes of worship and forty-minute sermon was added a concluding twenty minutes of worship. This later segment afforded involvement in participatory art projects arranged around the auditorium.

The Rhythm of Discipleship and the Word

Dan Kimball is motivated by two theoretical concepts. The first is the Great Commission of Matthew 28:19-20, which Kimball sees reflected in Vintage Faith's goal of "attracting those who normally would never consider Christianity or even desire to be part of a church community." [4]

The second motivation comes from an unlikely source, Mahatma Gandhi, who Kimball quotes as saying, "I like your Christ, but don't like your Christians. Your Christians are so unlike your Christ." This critique motivates Kimball to encourage attendees to live an altruistic life of both testimony and service to the community.

Subsequently, Vintage Faith refers to its congregation as "a worshiping community of missional theologians." This last term initially disturbed me, probably because only recently did I finish paying my seminary bills. But Vintage Faith employs this appellation because it reminds congregants that they must conduct theological inspection and reflection, grappling with the good news' implications for their neighbors. Thus, I have come to respect and appreciate the term.

Their "missional" orientation is also shared with other organic churches. "Being 'missional' simply means to be outward and others-focused with the goals of expressing and sharing the love of Jesus," states Kimball. "The church was not created for itself to remain inward-focused, but actually created to worship God and to spread his love to others. . . . Therefore, we don't have a 'missions department' because the whole church is a mission." [5] And, though the environs were innovative in ambiance and décor, the theology was in keeping with a Bible Church perspective.

Inspired Rhythms

Inspired Rhythms of Place

Vintage Faith excels in creating sacred spaces, brimming with symbolism, ancient-future ambiance,[6] and an unpretentious yet reverential mood. The ability to do so in the conventional atmosphere of a gymnasium is even more remarkable. This rhythm of place will be discussed more fully in the lesson section.

Inspired Rhythms of Worship

Often you will find painters or sculptors working and worshiping during worship gatherings, since Vintage Faith encourages artists of all mediums to participate in their worship expressions.[7] Subsequently, they have launched an artist-in-residence program, to allow vocational artists to mentor budding artists, to design art for the worship expressions, and to be mentored themselves. Though an artist-in-residence program is customary in universities, civic organizations, and some mainline churches, it is refreshing to see a missional church use more than the musical arts to worship God as well as to reach the community.

Inspired Rhythms of Discipleship and the Word

Due to a passion intelligently and conscientiously to engage their neighbors, Vintage Faith offers what they call a school of theology. Though unaccredited, this school's purpose is to create theological as well as practical learning environments for congregants. Classes meet once a week for six weeks to cover topics such as "The Story of the Church" (church history) and "Tapestry of Faiths in Santa Cruz" (examining the city's religious mosaic).

Finally, Vintage Faith makes a deliberate effort to be a multigenerational church.[8] They purposely do not schedule conflicting generational events, and they offer numerous intergenerational opportunities. Though this is often talked about, even lauded in the organic church, it is rarely practiced with such veracity as at Vintage Faith.

An Interview with My Tour Guide

Dan Kimball (*pastor*)

Where did the idea of sacred spaces come from?
It came from working with youth at a large contemporary Bible church for ten years. It was alive and growing with older people, but not with many in their twenties. They met in a large contemporary multipurpose room, employing contemporary praise songs and high application preaching. Art, liturgy, and other more ancient forms of worship were not used. And there wasn't too much time allotted to praying and slowing down.

Yet, when I asked younger Christians and non-Christians about what they wanted in a church, ironically many of them wanted "church to feel more like a church." They wanted the meeting place to have crosses, an architectural feel that communicated a sense of worship, and times of quiet in addition to the times of upbeat worship. Some told me that church was feeling like a professional motivational presentation, like a Tony Robbins seminar. Instead, they wanted a place where they could quiet their hearts and encounter God. So we looked at the Bible and began to see that worship throughout the Bible involved more than just upbeat one-way preaching and singing. Subsequently, we've endeavored to create authentic worship encounters, to build community, and to provide sacred spaces where people could go off and pray.

You make artists an integral part of creating these sacred spaces. Why?

In many contemporary churches, artists are ignored. Instead, churches have developed sports metaphors, with teams and coaches. And pastors are often the athletic type. This resonates with a lot of people, and that's okay. But artists and a lot of other people don't necessarily relate to sports. In addition, the modern church is centered around speaking and music, but God has given many artists other expressions. At Vintage Faith, artists design prayer stations. Each station has a scripture and a creative way to interact and pray with the Scriptures that are being employed in the sermon.

You were on the staff of a large church. How did you make the transition?

We got together a group of leaders and began to pray about it. We decided to host an art event called "Frames," and we invited photographers, sculptors, painters, and so on. At that time, about six hundred people came to our church's young adult worship gathering. I thought we might have twelve or fifteen artists. We had over sixty artists show up! I had no idea this person was a sculptor, or that one was a photographer. They were around us all the time, but no one had given them an opportunity to share their God-given art. We invited them to help us think through and design our worship gatherings.

Do you have any advice for a church that is trying to create a sacred space in a gymnasium or multipurpose facility?
The key is to get a group of volunteers in their twenties and thirties excited about this. A lot of young people are good at art. So let them come up with the design of what to do for ambiance. In the beginning, I gave them some examples and took them to some websites to show how other churches are addressing this. That helped them get a picture, but they took it from there and created spaces that were reflective of our community. Worship is like an artist's pallette. It's a place where God mixes various gifts and talents to form a beautiful expression of worship.

Three Lessons to Consider

Lesson 1

Let sacred spaces support your mission. There was nothing wrong with the aesthetics of the Santa Cruz Bible Church auditorium, for it carried the feel of a conference center or a lecture hall. A boomer predilection for such venues may be due to an emphasis on the church's teaching role. However, the lighting, art, mood walls, candles, prayer cove, and so on at Vintage Faith may indicate a Generation X preference for balancing head and heart. Vintage Faith created a powerful and encircling atmosphere of mystery, wonder, learning, and supernatural encounter.

The following are some of the ways Vintage Faith creates sacred spaces:[9]

Curtains make the institutional feel of a multipurpose auditorium more intimate and private. Though Vintage Faith worships in an auditorium that will hold seven hundred-plus, the encircling curtains help attendees feel they are in a private and personal encounter with God.

Prayer areas are created between the curtains and the outer walls. Large throw pillows, candles, and rugs not only create a 270-degree cocoon of prayer, but also keep prayer a focus.

A prayer cove beyond an arched trellis offers a space for extended times of prayer with intercessors. I have observed that over time a

47

prayer room's proximity to the platform can wane, paralleling a distancing of prayer from centrality in a growing congregation.[10] Vintage Faith avoids this by placing their prayer cove near the stage.

Seating includes tables as well as rows of chairs. Tables allow interaction for those desiring it, while forward facing chairs allow other attendees a degree of anonymity.

The platform was off center, so that a large cross was centered in the auditorium expressing the centrality of Jesus. Consequently, musicians and the lectern were not centrally located, nor were they the focus.

Low lighting and candles create a sense of reverence, expectation, and mystery. The candles are also "symbolic of Jesus as the light of the world," stated Kimball. Though lighting was raised slightly during the sermon so notes could be taken, their muted luminosity kept the focus off the leaders, the audience, and other extraneous distractions.

Two mood walls were some of the more creative elements. To create these, the end walls of the auditorium were left bare above the eight-foot-high curtaining. On the white wall above, video projectors slowly and appropriately beamed images correlating to the theme of the night. This worked remarkably well, creating a 270-degree experience (the rear wall was not used).

Art of diverse mediums was displayed on the stage and around the room. Large paintings in genres ranging from classic to Postimpressionism ringed the room. In addition, congregants were encouraged to participate in interactive artwork, which during my visit included a large mosaic that would upon completion be displayed in the auditorium.

A final caveat. These examples should serve as models to assist others in sketching their own indigenized elements. They are not to be followed unswervingly, but rather used as examples to forge a coalition between church leaders and artists.

Lesson 2

Engage and mentor artists of varied mediums. Artistic expression is a reflection of God's creative power and love. And Kimball points to Genesis 1 and Exodus 31:3-4 to suggest that creativity is "ingrained in who we are." Though the modern church has long recognized the applicability of musical arts, it has been slow to effectively use other artistic mediums. The organic church, however, is serving as an experimental milieu for a fusion of artistic mediums. Thus, canvas one's congregation, and then, with artistically imbued individuals, dream up avenues to use their talents in worship and in outreach.

Out of such brainstorming, Vintage Faith developed an artist-in-residence program. This not only provides for the physical needs of struggling artists, but also assists them in becoming what Vintage Faith calls "missional theologians." Here is how the program has developed at Vintage Faith:

A portfolio review is required for entrance into the program. It is open to filmmakers, actors, designers, curators, photographers, visual artists, sculptors, painters, and so on.

Selection is based upon a desire to advance their artistic medium, a Christian commitment, and a devotion to foster talent and engagement in both churched and unchurched people.

Responsibilities include mentoring developing artists in the congregation through classes, dialogue, and tutoring. In addition, they contribute to artistic expressions during worship gatherings and in the civic community. One artist organized a downtown art event at Easter, including twelve stations of the cross, each created by different artists.

Support includes mentoring by the pastoral staff, raw materials, and the opportunity to add to their portfolio. Though no remuneration is given, a trip to the Christians in Vocational Arts (CIVA) convention has been included.

Such artist-in-residence programs may be necessary to redirect modern overemphasis on the musical arts and to restore a full gamut of creative arts to their rightful prominence and usefulness in the body of Christ.

Lesson 3

Create multigenerational (Multi-gen.) communities. Scriptures such as Titus 2:3-5 presuppose a multigenerational milieu, in which mature Christians have a responsibility and opportunity to pass along life lessons and values to younger generations. Anthropologist Margaret Mead's research revealed that faith and values better transfer down from grandparents to grandchild than from parent to child, concluding, "It is true that continuity of all cultures depends on the living presence of at least three generations."[11] Thus, intergenerational proximity in a world in which biological grandparents live increasingly far away means the church must foster a Multi-gen. environment for the transmission of spiritual beliefs.

In my earlier writings, I pointed out that an inability to reach out to younger generations without alienating older generations is the primary killer of churches in America.[12] To thwart this malady, congregations must embrace, as Vintage Faith embraces, a missional philosophy that includes reaching out to multiple generations concurrently. Toward this end, my earlier writings describe seven steps that will help almost any church grow into a healthy Multi-gen. congregation.[13]

However, for this present discussion, let me share a few Multi-gen. insights:

(1) **Involve all age groups in your core leadership.** Kimball explains that "our core leadership will be comprised of those of all ages . . . [for] we desire to see a broad age span of those who are part of the Vintage Faith community."

(2) **Do not schedule conflicting generational events.** Although there are age-specific ministries, the leadership of Vintage Faith scrutinizes the schedule to ensure families are together as much as feasible.

(3) **Create opportunities for older congregants to disciple and share with younger congregants.** Both social theory and the Bible confirm that grandparent-age congregants will be especially helpful in imparting values and belief systems to persons the age of their grandchildren attendees. "A very high value in this church will be older generations mentoring and discipling the younger," reflects Kimball.

CHAPTER 6

Freeway
Baton Rouge, Louisiana

Through films, television, books, and the like, history and past experience are turned into a seemingly vast archive "instantly retrievable." . . . The postmodern penchant for jumbling together all manner of references to past styles is one of its more pervasive characteristics.

—David Harvey, professor and author[1]

First Encounters

The road that a young organic church called Freeway took me down was not what I expected, for the sermon careened in a surprising direction. The first half was an analysis of film clips from young comedians and their perspective on modern culture. Often stopping the playback, Steve, the pastor, asked attendees to yell out the next line from the movies, and a rousing chorus reminded me that these people were well-acquainted with the philosophy these young comedians espoused. But Steve didn't stop there; he soon juxtaposed the message in these movies with the Word of God and thoughtfully demonstrated where they converged and where they diverged.

Dashboard

Church: Freeway
Leaders: Steve Wallace (pastor), David Loti (worship leader)
Location: Prairieville, Louisiana; a suburb of Baton Rouge
Affiliation: Nondenominational

Size: 65+

Audience: Artists, postmoderns, multiple generations, and pre-Christians–people who are spiritually sensitive

Website: www.freewaybr.com

A Fusion of Rhythms

Shared Rhythms

The Rhythm of Place

The environment at Freeway reminded me of many other organic churches. The auditorium was lit only with candles, and refreshments were available and enjoyed throughout the evening. Informal gatherings of young people milled around the auditorium enjoying one another's fellowship so much that few save your author noticed that the worship service started twenty-five minutes late. An unhurried, but communal feel pervaded this church even before the worship celebration began.

The Rhythm of Worship

The worship also mirrored what I had seen in many organic congregations. The worship leaders eschewed all sense of artificial and synthetic trappings, commencing worship with an earnest and humble song of spiritual longing. In the low light of a myriad of candles, the simple words of spiritual yearning, hunger, and need pierced my heart as deeply as the song leader's plain if irregular vocalization. His vocal interpretation accompanied by a simple guitar rendered the words even more poignant and piercing. Within minutes, this worship celebration led me into an encounter with my own fickle heart and with a generous God who looks beyond my inadequacies.

Inspired Rhythms

Inspired Rhythms of Discipleship and the Word

Steve Wallace's topic that night was "Why do we laugh at other people?" and his message began with a look at what he called "the four voices of our generation." Expecting to hear homilies by poets, philosophers, or lyricists, I was surprised when on the screen appeared the faces of comedians Jim Carrey, Ben Stiller, Adam Sandler, and Will Farrell. "These are the people who are telling you what to think" continued Steve, "and I want you to understand what they're saying."

For the next twenty-five minutes Steve dissected some of the funniest scenes I have ever witnessed. Steve pointed out that though hilarious, each scene depicted a way that people often heap ego-driven humiliation upon less fortunate people. After a few minutes I was embarrassed to laugh at these depictions, even though they brimmed with hilarity. Steve had helped me see something deeper, that these scenarios were often crafted at the expense of the less fortunate and were creating a youth culture less sensitive and compassionate.

Launching into a lesson supported with biblical texts, Steve argued that Jesus stands in solidarity with the disenfranchised. Steve skillfully turned the topic from the comedic vignettes of urban legend to the lasting principles of God's Word, which call us to demonstrate compassion and action toward the disadvantaged.

At the conclusion, I wondered how the message might have been driven home had Steve not commenced with film clips. In fact, his choice of comedic clips had led me to be subtly swept away by my more impious desire to laugh at others' expense. As a result, the lesson came home more convincingly than I expected it would.

In addition, I had been guided by this sermon into a deeper look into the intersection of culture and God's Word. The topic reminded me that a cross-cultural communicator must cautiously study and sift culture, being wary not to be corrupted by it, but being engaged enough to understand it as a missionary might understand a foreign way of life.

An Interview with My Tour Guide

Steve Wallace (*pastor*)

Why do you use film clips?
I was trying to connect with young people in my sermons, to make an intersection. And they all know these films. I don't mean to offend, but Adam Sandler, Ben Stiller, Will Farrell, and Jim Carey are the four evangelists of our time. There is a reason why the young people know whole passages of dialogue from their movies; because they are addressing the big issues of life, death, purpose, and the future. If we are going to explain biblical truths to young people, we must understand their beliefs and where they came from.

What was the result?
My research into these movies led to a twelve-sermon series that dealt with loyalty, friendship, leadership, trust, family, stress, anger, the future, and God. Adam, Ben, Will, and Jim often produce, write, and direct; and what they present is their take on life. We have to sift though this, and not just accept everything. And we also have to understand and affirm the stuff that is valid.

What did you find applicable in these movies?
Movies such as *The Majestic, The Truman Show,* and *Eternal Sunshine of the Spotless Mind* are disturbing films that cause you to look hard at spiritual issues. For example, Adam Sandler's film *50 First Dates* with Drew Barrymore has a powerful closing scene that demonstrates unconditional love. Drew has brain damage and can't recall short-term memories. Adam Sandler falls in love with her but each day has to reintroduce himself. She is an artist and one day takes him to her studio, which is full of portraits of him. She realizes that though she can't remember it, he has been an integral part of her life and essence. What a wonderful picture of how God paints knowledge of him into our lives.

Any parting advice?
Yes, I don't think you should take film clips out of context. I personally find it offensive when people take scriptures out of context. So I make sure I let my audience know I understand what Adam, Ben, Will, and Jim are trying to say. This gives me a degree of integrity with my audience. I'm not there to trash their stars. But I am there to make a point, and that is the Word of God has the answers to many of the questions that these comedians are asking.

Three Lessons to Consider

Lesson 1

Carefully investigate and examine elements of a culture. Since modern culture is constantly adjusting and metamorphosing, the task of translating the good news without surrendering its truth or disfiguring it is paramount and ongoing. This arduous task begins with thorough and careful examination of a culture. Anthropologist Paul Hiebert described culture as "an integrated system of learned patterns of behavior, ideas and products characteristic of a society."[2] Scrutiny of such an elaborate system is not for an immature Christian, since it requires investigating and evaluating a culture without being tainted by its more sordid elements.

However, a failure by Christian communicators to sufficiently investigate modern culture can make us look irrelevant. In an earlier book, I interviewed Larry Osborne, pastor of North Coast Church in Vista, California. Larry told me the phenomenal growth of his church was in part because he regularly studies modern culture by perusing secular business, entertainment, and lifestyle magazines. "If I don't understand the business world, when a businessperson talks to me about his or her world, it's like we're using two different dictionaries."[3] The use of disparate dictionaries can also dilute an exchange of ideas with any culture.

Therefore, stay current with today's postmodern culture by cautiously scrutinizing their books, music, movies, music videos, computer games, websites, blogs, and so on. Although the truths of the good news must never be sacrificed or altered, relating and contrasting the truths of the good news with today's culture can make the good news more comprehensible.

Lesson 2

Sift happens! Sift elements of a culture. There is a tension between Christ and culture that must be examined. H. Richard Niebuhr, in his classic treatise *Christ and Culture,* suggested that there are several ways to look at Christ's interaction with culture.[4]

One is "Christ against culture," a view embraced by the early church father Tertullian. In this view, culture is seen as evil, thus requiring Christians to withdraw and insulate themselves, resulting in a monastic response. Charles Kraft exposes three fallacies in this view, demonstrating it is not in keeping with Paul's view that "nothing is unclean in itself" (Romans 14:14 NRSV).[5]

Another view Niebuhr called "Christ above Culture," which he divided into subcategories.[6] "Christ above Culture in Synthesis" was held by Thomas Aquinas and views Jesus as the restorer of institutions of true society. This view believes that Christianity will one day totally transform culture, perhaps into a millennial peace. In another subcategory, "Christ above Culture in Paradox," Christ is seen above but in such tension with culture that a messy, muddled relationship results. Martin Luther grappled with this perspective, as did modern writer Mike Yaconelli who called this "messy spirituality."[7]

However, a more valid subcategory may be "Christ above but Transformer of Culture." Embraced by Augustine, John Calvin, and John Wesley, this view sees culture as corrupt but convertible.[8] Kraft built upon this with his position called "Christ above but Working Through Culture," explaining that "God chooses the cultural milieu in which humans are immersed as the arena of his interaction with people."[9] Eddie Gibbs further elaborates that "such an approach represents a deliberate self-limiting on the part of God in order to speak in understandable terms and with perceived relevance on the part of the hearer. He acts redemptively with regard to culture, which includes judgment on some elements, but also affirmation in other areas, and a transformation of the whole."[10]

If the "Christ above but Working Through Culture" truly defines the tension and nexus between Christ and culture, then the job of the Christian communicator becomes challenging, if not precarious. Therefore, our strategy must not conclude simply with step 1, investigating and examining culture, but also must continue through step 2, sifting and judging its elements. Here the prudent communicator must make qualitative judgments based upon Scripture, ethics, personal belief, and the guidance of the Holy Spirit.

Lesson 3

Reject or affirm elements of a culture. The end result of this examination or sifting must be a rejection of elements in conflict with Christ, and also an affirmation of those elements that are not in conflict. I found that leaders of the organic church usually sift carefully through the movies, television shows, music, games, online resources, and literature of young people. And they routinely explain in their sermons how God judges some aspects of postmodern culture, accepts other elements such as an emphasis on helping the needy, and has as a goal the transformation of the whole.[11]

The Christian communicator wishing to make the good news relevant today must carefully examine the media barrage engulfing young people and understand its messages, while at the same time sifting through elements that are opposed to Christ and identifying touchstones that can make connections with unchurched people.

CHAPTER 7

Church of the Apostles
Seattle, Washington

Theology is being done today—in curious places, under unusual sponsorship, by unauthorized persons, unnoticed by those who read only the right journals.

—Harvey Cox, theologian and author[1]

First Encounters

" 'Organic' is a great word," responded curate Ryan Marsh to my book title. "Our liturgy is even organic because it's created by a team and not only flows out of our various traditions, but also out of our various talents, tastes, and experiences. We're organic in many ways." However, I wondered if a liturgy created by so many voices might retain cohesiveness.

I was pleasantly surprised by the outcome. The liturgy unfolded in a unified and engaging manner. Each segment was led by a different person but carried forward the evening's theme. And tonight's theme was change, for Church of the Apostles (or COTA, or just Apostles) was moving to larger facilities across the street.

Dashboard

Church: Church of the Apostles
Leaders: Karen M. Ward (pastor), Tony Rivera (senior warden), Lacey Brown (music director), Ryan Marsh (curate)
Location: The Fremont neighborhood of Seattle, Washington

Affiliations: Evangelical Lutheran Church of America and the Episcopal Church, USA
Size: 40-55
Audience: Urban artists, metropolitan residents, people who are spiritually sensitive, urban poor, and diverse social classes
Websites: www.apostleschurch.org; www.emergingchurch.org; www.fremontabbey.org

A Fusion of Rhythms

Shared Rhythms

The Rhythm of Place

COTA uses a tea bar/performance space to support their ministry, with artists drawn from the surrounding Fremont art community. "We have people coming to us," remarked Marsh. "We've developed a reputation for an inexpensive performance space for bands, film-makers, classical musicians, poets, and more. And they don't have to be Christian. We see this as our way of engaging our community."

Typically artists receive 75 percent of the cover charge (usually $5 per person), while COTA receives the remaining 25 percent, plus tea and coffee sales. The income covers the venue's expenses. COTA does not expect the performance space to pro-vide for staff salaries, since most salaries are furnished by the two linked denominations.

Inspired Rhythms

Inspired Rhythms of Worship

COTA is a self-described *ancient-future* church. "Ancient-future speaks to postmodern generations," stated Ward. "It draws equally upon ancient (hymns, chants, candles, communion) as well as techno-modern sources (alternative rock, art, ambiance, projections, video). So there is no need to 'check your culture at the door.' "[2]

This ancient-future orientation has helped COTA connect with people accustomed to liturgical expressions, but also to those who long for an authentic encounter with God.[3] Again Marsh put it well: "I graduated with a Biblical Studies degree, but I was too evangelical for many mainline churches and too liturgical for evangelical churches. COTA is both."

Here is an annotated liturgy from COTA.

(1) **Opening words/welcome/greeting.** Marsh, from a microphone in the rear of the auditorium, and music director Lacey Brown, perched behind a drum set, invited everyone to share their name and the last trip they took.

(2) **Song:** "Walk On" by a six-piece band.

(3) Marsh introduced the **confession,** explaining, "We often don't feel right about leaving, until we've made things 'right.' "

(4) **Absolution.**

(5) **Psalm drumming.** Psalm 89:1-4 was read (focusing on God's steadfastness in the midst of change), accompanied by dozens of drums, some played from the stage, others by audience members.

(6) **Gospel reading:** Matthew 10:40-42.

(7) **Reverb** was an articulate and engaging sermon by Karen Ward, who began, "I wore this T-shirt because on it is one of my favorite R.E.I. scriptures [referring to the wilderness outfitter]. It says 'Not all who wander are lost.' "

(8) **Song:** "Yahweh"

(9) **Open Space** is a time for contemplation and reflection. Large sheets of paper allowed people to journal their memories from two years in this facility.

(10) **Prayer huddles** of three to four people were created.

(11) **The Peace** was shared.

(12) **The Eucharist** was offered from a backpack, meant to symbolize their journey.

(13) **Song:** "Agnus Dei"

(14) **Family business** included announcements.

(15) **Sending ritual** included packing the suitcase with the Eucharist and journal sheets.

(16) **Sending song:** "Those Who Trust"

(17) **Dismissal**

(18) **Postlude:** "Walk On"

Inspired Rhythms of Discipleship and the Word

The name, Church of the Apostles, was chosen not only to specify a church built only on the teachings of ancient prelates, but also to emphasize that all Christians are called to bear the role of "apostles."[4] Karen Ward states, "The first small group that got up and went with Jesus got tagged 'apostles,' from a Greek word that means 'those sent out.' Because they went with Jesus, he blessed and sent them to carry on in his way of living and to welcome others to do the same. The invitation still stands. . . . Apostles are regular people who hear God calling and decide to answer."[5] COTA imbues the term with a sense of the responsibility, wisdom, and duty of all missional Christians.

COTA also seeks to dialogue with the viewpoints of those it reaches, for the relativistic and postmodern philosophy of many Fremont residents differs from COTA's belief in biblical truth. Apostle thus creates an image of not only going out, but also logically engaging a community. As Cambridge professor Simon Blackburn cautions, we must "resist being slaves of simplistic relativism or equally simplistic absolutisms. . . . Whichever way our temperaments pull us, we should at least know what there is to be said on the other side."[6] COTA's perspective is that an apostle practices this.

An Interview with My Tour Guide

Karen Ward (*pastor*)

You have been called an authority on the organic church. How did this happen?
I was serving as an official in the Lutheran Church but didn't have a church where I felt my unchurched 20- and 30-something friends could go. My ideal church would include ancient and

modern elements. I found an outlet when I started a website called emergingchurch.org. I began to dialogue with people around the globe who thought the same crazy things I did: that a church could be ancient and future as well as spiritually relevant, at the same time.

COTA is engaged in the community. Can you describe some ways?

We live in an art community, so we're highly involved in supporting art and artists. We're creating the Fremont Abbey, an art/performance space across from our old location. I call it a monastic/artistic venue because we will practice Christian spiritual formation there through disciplines in prayer, service, reflection, and study. But we'll also engage community artists with a restaurant, performance venues, and studios. We want to do what is native to our culture, and art is the soul of this neighborhood.

You employ what could be described as an organic liturgy. How do you do this?

We are trying to speak the Word of God, which is ancient, to a world that is grappling with today and the future. So we're continually and carefully creating liturgy, to ensure it connects people with God. To do this we make sure it is the result of everything that is happening to us during the week. Wednesday night is about planning, but all week long God is preparing, and the liturgy is brewing. Our planning meeting is the culmination of the brew.

Three Lessons to Consider

Lesson 1

Balance an **ancient-future** *orientation to reach people who appreciate liturgical expressions.* A structured order of worship, when permeated with modern artistic elements, can help create a nexus between well-founded historical practices (ancient) and techno-modern artistic forms (future). Here is a brief, yet incomplete, comparison of ancient-future components.

Figure 4. A Partial Comparison of Ancient-Future Elements[7]

An *Ancient-Future* Orientation
Fuses the Two

	Ancient	Future
Liturgical Musicology	—Hymns —Chants, etc. —Professional interpretation	—Alternative music —Drum circles, etc. —Audience participation
Ambiance	—Candles —Natural lighting	—Computerized images —Mood walls
Iconography	—Plain icons such as: • Ichthus symbol • Chi Rho (Constantinian) cross • Lavishly ornamented icons such as: • Celtic symbols and crosses • Byzantine symbols and crosses	—Techno-icons such as: • Mars Hill's Directions© signs • St. Tom's Lifeshapes© • Stylized icons, where artists interpret ancient symbols through modern artistic genres, e.g. multi-media, expressionism, surrealism, kinetic art, etc.
Truth Delivery	—Presentation of the Word through sermonizing, pedagogy	—Interaction with the Word through questioning and dialogue —Native[8] musical lyrics

	—Intricate musical lyrics —Art, such as stained glass windows, mosaics, sculpture, church architecture, banners/tapestries, drama, etc. —Stations of the Cross	—Art, such as film, video, acting, design, poetry, dance, photography, pottery, visual arts, abstract art, kinetic art, mixed-mediums, and so on —Interactive stations
Christ and Culture	—Christ Against Culture[9] leads to monastic disciplines (e.g. Tertullian, St. Benedict): • Prayer grottos • Prayer labyrinths • Meditation • Spiritual retreat	—Christ above but Working Through Culture[10] leads to *sifting* culture in which, • Some elements are judged • Others are reaffirmed • For the transformation of the whole[11]
Discipleship Ethos	—Monastic, "withdrawal from the institutions and societies of civilization"[12]	—Missional, with engagement and "dynamic equivalence"[13]

Regrettably, churches often expunge liturgical elements in the name of flexibility or modernization. However, COTA demonstrates that a liturgical expression can build upon the familiarity and strengths of the past, incorporate the best of the present-future, with the result of a convincing spiritual encounter. As Eddie Gibbs stated,

> The innovative leader does not destroy all that he has inherited as an essential prerequisite for a successful investment in the future. He is appreciative of the insights and achievements of previous

generations, and possesses discernment to identify those elements which are of lasting value. He is also aware that the "latest" does not necessarily equate with the "best."[14]

An ancient-future approach may also be attractive to people whose initial faith experience occurred in a liturgical milieu. Years of consulting have led me to believe that Christians have high positive regard for the artistic forms that accompanied their first encounter with Christ. Thus, if a person encountered Christ in an Anglican or Lutheran congregation, their preference for spiritual encounter later in life might be in more liturgical environs.[15]

Lesson 2

Use organic involvement (such as many voices) in the creation of your liturgical expressions. COTA creates their liturgical structure in a Wednesday evening session open to a wide range of congregational voices. In addition, the liturgy is created to reflect the faith journey the community has experienced that week.

Such organic initiation is needed, since oftentimes liturgy is created by the same few people each week. Such limited and repetitious participation can drain liturgy of its freshness and creativity. Thus, the organic involvement of many voices and their community experience ensure that liturgy does not become stale or pedestrian.

Lesson 3

Build your persuasion upon proclamation and presence. COTA's mission is to meet the needs of the community, lucidly explain the good news to them, and then credibly explain the dissimilarities and similarities between postmodern and Christian viewpoints. Many churches, however, get stuck in one phase of this three-stage process. Let's look at a graph that explains the building-block nature of cultural engagement.

Figure 5. Building an Organic Home of P-1, P-2, and P-3 Evangelism[16]

Apostles are found in all levels

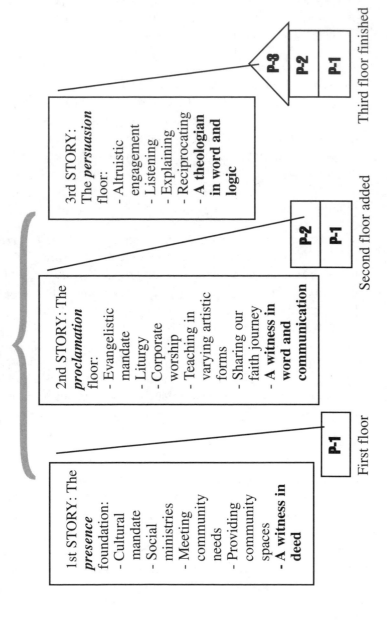

1st STORY: The *presence* foundation:
- Cultural mandate
- Social ministries
- Meeting community needs
- Providing community spaces
- **A witness in deed**

2nd STORY: The *proclamation* floor:
- Evangelistic mandate
- Liturgy
- Corporate worship
- Teaching in varying artistic forms
- Sharing our faith journey
- **A witness in word and communication**

3rd STORY: The *persuasion* floor:
- Altruistic engagement
- Listening
- Explaining
- Reciprocating
- **A theologian in word and logic**

P-1

P-2

P-1

P-3

P-2

P-1

First floor

Second floor added

Third floor finished

A **presence foundation** (P-1) means that all communication is first built upon the cultural mandate of meeting human needs.[17]

Proclamation (P-2) is our cogent and relevant explanation of the claims of Christ that is built upon a firm foundation of presence.

Finally, the persuasion level (P-3) only rises once we have built supporting structures. It is here where keen cultural insights meet persuasive knowledge. The term "persuasion" is apt, for the New Testament often employs the Greek word *peitho*, meaning "to persuade, bring about a change of mind by the influence of reason or moral considerations."[18]

Think of figure 5 as a residence, with people of varying giftings and maturities living communally. Some will be more skilled at presence evangelism, and thus they may reside on the first floor, interacting with those on the street and who pass by. In similar fashion, there are those equipped by God and circumstance to elucidate the good news in modern language. These are communicators in word and art. They live on the second floor, explaining the good news to those who the first-floor residents welcome in.

And those who live on the upper floor gain a wider picture of the world. They see further and more theologically.[19] They understand the world both near and far and engage it mentally, artistically, and logically.[20] They are the philosophers and thinkers, sifting culture for the transformation of the whole.

Therefore, only once the visitor has experienced our house through presence, explanation, and finally logic are they able holistically and organically to respond to our entire effort, that is, our organic dwelling.

And so in our home many people live on different floors as they are gifted and called. But we are all one house, living in a synergetic relationship of dependence. Thus, to the world outside we exist as a completed and authentic structure, not as an unfinished edifice.

CHAPTER 8

One Place
Phoenix, Arizona

A contemporary church, like a contemporary translation, should impress the uninitiated observer as an original production in the contemporary culture, not as a badly fitted import from somewhere else.

—*Charles Kraft, anthropologist and author*[1]

First Encounters

The preacher was nervous, for One Place Church had not had regular sermons for over a year, and this was his audition. Dressed in floppy hat, t-shirt, and faded jeans, he delivered a remarkably poignant and engaging sermon, sprinkled with video clips from current movies.

As I sat in the middle of more than seventy attendees, I wondered how this church had survived for over a year without a teaching pastor or regular sermons. "Without a teaching pastor, we had to teach the Word though mediums other than the spoken word," stated Mark, the senior pastor and worship leader. "Interactive stations became our primary means for truth delivery." Looking at the vibrant and enthusiastic throng, it appeared to work.

Dashboard

Church: One Place Church
Leaders: Mark Roberts (senior pastor and worship leader), Jill Roberts (administrator and hospitality), Adam Brooks (outreach ministry), Israel Whittemore (worship ministries), Katie Whittemore (prayer and counseling ministries)

Location: Phoenix, Arizona
Affiliations: Nondenominational, but started by another organic church, Highway Community Church in Palo Alto, California
Size: 50-75
Audience: People in their twenties into mid-thirties, artists, metropolitan residents, homeless and urban poor, service industry workers, college/postmodern thinkers, and diverse social classes throughout and around Phoenix, Arizona
Website: www.oneplacechurch.com

A Fusion of Rhythms

Shared Rhythms

The Rhythm of Place

Though the church was meeting in a suburban school, candles, artwork, and low lights were employed to transform the school theatre into a serene and reverential clime, imbued with a sense of the mystery and wonder of God. And similar to The Bridge, One Place has recently moved into the inner city to be nearer to the people who are homeless, poor, and disenfranchised and with whom they feel solidarity.[2]

The Rhythm of Worship

Though dozens of stage lights hung from the ceiling, the stage was lit only with candles scattered across the stage. Again, there is a propensity in the organic church to let the unprocessed luminance of nature's light create both expectation as well as adulation.

The worship also carried a decidedly authentic and transformational timbre. Leaders told me they had been burned out in a perceived quest for professionalism in their parents' churches. But they were quick to point out that though burned out on their parents' religiosity, they were not burned out on their religion. Subsequently, they sought to create a more stress-free and *laissez-faire* spiritual encounter.

The Rhythm of Discipleship and the Word

One Place embraces a missional perspective wed with an orthodox evangelical theology. Their following "guiding values"[3] represent well those embraced by many organic churches.

Authentic community. The connection with our Creator opens the way for real relationships. In our journey together, being real is more important than appearing good.

Transforming love. We love people wholeheartedly and sacrificially, pursuing the transformation of individuals and our community.

Holistic worship. True worship is more than mere singing; it is a transformational encounter with the living God. We will pour out our lives in corporate worship and individual acts of praise.

Endless mission. The church doesn't exist for itself. We are lifelong missionaries, laying down our lives for the sake of those who are still seeking.

Soul revolution. God wants to overthrow our old way of life; we will not be satisfied with how far we've come. We will continue to push into God and will help others do the same.

Inspired Rhythms

Inspired Rhythms of Discipleship and the Word

Interactive stations, sort of interactive and artistically orientated stations of the cross,[4] have usually been considered under rhythms of worship. However, these stations can serve as channels for the transmission of the Word, even though they are often relegated to a supporting role for worship. Yet because of necessity, One Place employed these interactive stations as the primary mechanisms for what Mark Roberts calls "truth delivery." In other words, interactive stations had to serve as the main message carriers for the year-long period in which the church was without a teaching pastor.

My visit coincided with the end of this year, and I was surprised to see a maturity and spiritual growth in the congregation, even though truth delivery had been primarily through interactive stations. Examples of One Place's interactive stations will be explored in the section "Three Lessons to Consider."

An Interview with My Tour Guide

Mark Roberts (*senior pastor and worship leader*)

Without a teaching pastor, you relied upon interactive stations as the main avenues for truth delivery. How did this come about?

Every mainstream church has a teaching pastor, so we felt we had a hole to fill. But when our leaders filled the gap, we were really mediocre because it wasn't our giftings. We asked ourselves, "What are all the ways God speaks to us?" We concluded that the thirty-minute sermon is only one way and that there are other ways God can deliver truth. So is the teaching portion really a gap, or should we emphasize the things we are strong in, such as in the arts? It's more native. It's who we are. And we do it passionately.

How do you structure this?

We do an eight-week series on one theme, with different topics each week. We plan each week's stations in advance to support the theme and topic. We make sure they have scriptural support and lessons you can apply. We also give the congregation specific direction; we don't want to say, "Hey, go figure that station out on your own." We explain the foundational topic, back it up with scripture, and describe each station. During the interactive time, we worship, and we allow attendees to share scripture, poetry, or a short story about the topic.

What has this taught you about the advantage of interactive stations?

It reinforces the idea that God longs to teach us though different gifts in the body of Christ. And when the whole church body is involved, we see powerful experiences with Christ.

Three Lessons to Consider

Lesson 1

Create interactive stations to enhance your truth delivery. One Place demonstrates that interactive stations can play a more vital role than just supporting our musical expressions. And although musical lyrics can be truth delivery conduits, so can poetry, journaling, painting, and sculpture. Therefore, look to your interactive stations not as antidotes to boredom, but as compelling message carriers. Don't relegate them to second-class status, rather see them as full partners in God's creative and redemptive mission.

To understand creative and proficient truth delivery stations, the following are stations employed by One Place:

Community art stations. Here attendees participate in the creation of a work of art. In one example, each person received a unique ribbon. An empty frame was positioned so that congregants could stop, pray, and add their ribbon to the developing montage. "Everybody would uniquely weave in their ribbon," recalled Mark. "And, at the end we had a beautiful tapestry of ribbons." The topic, belonging to a community while also being unique, was supported by 1 Corinthians 12:1-31 and Ephesians 4:7-13.

Labyrinths. Labyrinths of complex circular paths have historically been used by the Christian church to foster spiritual contemplation. One Place adds mini-stations along the route to emphasize scripture, prayer, dependence on Jesus, and even partaking in the Lord's Supper. This allows the labyrinth to function not simply as a meditative tool, but also as a teaching tool.

Confessional opportunities. Confession is a part of most churches' liturgy. But One Place deploys this element in creative ways. On one occasion, they asked attendees to confess their sins privately before God and then write them on a piece of paper. Attendees were then invited to bring them to an interactive station and lay them at the foot of a cross. However, the pens dispensed disappearing ink. "By the time they made it to the station, the sin was gone," recalled Mark. "We even saw people go back to their chair to rewrite the sin, only to see it disappear again." Another time, attendees were asked to paint on a large canvas something representing an area in which they were selfish. During the following week's worship an artist painted a picture of God's forgiveness and redemption over the entire canvas. And on another occasion, congregants wrote their sins down on a piece of paper and tied them to large rocks. The rocks were then thrown into a sizeable vat of water, where they sunk to the bottom beyond retrieval.

Resting in God's grace. One theme focused on not being so busy that we forget to stop, rest, and connect with God. One Place spread out pillows all around the auditorium and invited congregants to sit on the floor as they prayed and meditated on the scriptures provided. "Some worshiped, some prayed, and some even fell asleep," laughed Mark. "But it was a powerful lesson on not getting too busy, but taking time to experience God's rest."

Gift-sharing stations. Often in the organic church, artists are invited to create art during worship. For example, a painter might create a painting inspired by the music or topic.[5] One Place took this a step further, allowing artists to sometimes write songs during the service (staying in the same key as the singing). Then if the artists wish, they can share their composition.

Voices of the Holy Spirit. This station addressed the topic of envisioning God's plans, both corporately and individually. An isolated room became an interactive station in which attendees could anonymously use a voice recorder to record the vision that Christ was giving them. "We edited it quickly," stated Mark. "And then later in the service we replayed the recording for everyone, with music underneath it to disguise the voices."

Snapshots of God's presence. A month before Easter, disposable cameras were handed out and each person was given a different Easter theme to photograph. Topics included rejection, suffering, forgiveness, sacrifice, grace, resurrection, and rebirth. On Easter Sunday, the pictures were grouped in stations according to topic, with accompanying scriptures and a description of the lesson.

Lesson 2

Don't allow the spoken word to monopolize your teaching ministry. It is important to see varied communication mediums as not just suitable, but God-ordained conduits for truth delivery. The adage that a picture is worth a thousand words must not be lost on the church.

In addition, during periods of church history when illiteracy was common, pictorial representations of God's truth dominated the truth delivery process. During the Renaissance, paintings by Sandro Botticelli, Michelangelo Buonarroti, and Sanzio Raphael engaged nobleman and peasant alike with the grandeur, compassion, and magnificence of Christ's life and sacrifice. During the Reformation, ideologically dueling artists such as Rembrandt van Rijn and Peter Paul Rubens contended for Catholic or Reformation convictions in their art. And, describing how Saint Patrick reached the barbaric Celts of Ireland, George G. Hunter recalled, "They did not rely, as some traditions come close to, upon preaching alone to communicate the fullness of Christianity. They seem to have employed as many different 'media' as they could to get the message across, and to get people involved with the message."[6]

Only since the Enlightenment and especially in the twentieth century with an upsurge in avenues and outlets for the spoken word has oratory transmission of the good news been preferred. This may be to our detriment, allowing too much focus to be placed on narrow oral communication, and not on the plurality of message carriers God provides. A media fixation of Christians upon televised sermonizing may belie an unhealthy emphasis on a primary oral conduit for communication. However, Mel Gibson's creative and controversial *The Passion of the Christ* and Fuller Seminary's engagement with the film industry may be harbingers of a correction in course.

Thus, if we recognize the important role artists play historically and strategically in the communication of God's truth, we can help prevent overaggrandizement of the orator's role, as well as encourage communication through a mixture of transmission and artistic mediums.

Lesson 3

Create an indigenous values statement that encapsulates your beliefs, purpose, and focus. One Place's leaders developed a surprisingly succinct and lucid values statement during a late-night brainstorming session. Although many congregations simply borrow statements verbatim from other sources, creating your own can be more evocative.

The following is an approach that can foster innovation and creativity for the creation of such statements.[7]

(1) Select example statements.

(2) Prior to meeting together, ask leaders to read example statements as background.

(3) Join together to brainstorm.

Brainstorming guidelines[8]

—There is no discussion until after the brainstorming process.

—The more options the better.

—All ideas are welcome.

—Combinations of options are sought.

—Proposing or hearing an option does not mean accepting it.

Brainstorming elements[9]

—The leader describes the problem.

—Group members share their ideas. Clarification is allowed, but no one is allowed to criticize. Everyone withholds judgment until all alternatives have been heard.

—Only when all alternatives have been suggested do group members debate the merits of each.

(4) Team creates statement.

(5) Draft statement is distributed to attendees, volunteers, and colleagues.

(6) Modifications are requested.

(7) Leadership meets to codify statement.

(8) Statement is adopted.

Remember, a good statement creates an emotional bond and sense of mission between an organization and its participants.[10]

CHAPTER 9

Scum of the Earth Church Denver, Colorado

And I forget just why I taste. . . .
Oh well, whatever, nevermind.
—Kurt Cobain, Krist Novoselic, and Dave Grohl,
"Smells Like Teen Spirit,"
on the album Nevermind *by Nirvana[1]*

First Encounters

The parking lot was filled with urban youth playing basketball, skateboarding, smoking, or just hanging out. And while I have visited organic churches across North America and England, the congregation assembled here was one of the edgiest.

I entered the auditorium behind a young man with large earrings, tattoos, cropped hair, and a torn shirt. On the way I passed another young man dressed all in black with wild black-dyed hair. "We have a lot of Goths going here," reflected Mike Sares, copastor of the congregation, referring to the Gothic-styled young people. "They know they are accepted here even though they are different."

"And that guy with the large earrings," continued Eric, the other copastor, "he's a student from Denver Seminary. People here often look different, but among this group you'll find Christians and non-Christians. That's because we're a place to engage a segment of culture many churches ignore."

This congregation's outreach to young broad-minded urbanites is reflected in their name, a designation that has gained them some notoriety, and the rationale for which will be discussed shortly.

Dashboard

Church: Scum of the Earth Church
Leaders: Mike Sares and Eric Bain (copastors), E. J. Branch (pastor of The Refuse, a daughter congregation in Colorado Springs)
Location: Denver, Colorado
Affiliations: Nondenominational, though Mike Sares is ordained through the Alliance for Renewal, Eric Bain is seeking ordination with the Evangelical Covenant Church, and E. J. Branch is seeking ordination with the Christian Reformed Church.
Size: 350-400
Audience: Urban poor, homeless, disenfranchised youth, Goths, skateboarders, urban artists, immigrant families, blue-collar families, seminary students/professors, and diverse social classes throughout and around Denver
Website: www.scumoftheearth.net

A Fusion of Rhythms

Shared Rhythms

The Rhythm of Place

"It doesn't really fit us," mused Sares. "Our former location was better." "It was called The Toll Gate," reflected Bain, "an odd-looking building, right on Colfax. It's a tough section of town and isn't a place where you would start a church to reach lovely people." "But almost overnight we lost our lease," stated Sares. "And Church in the City was kind enough to let us come here. It's in the right neighborhood, but for us it has too much of a church feel."

A former grocery store, the facility had been converted into an urban boomer church by Church in the City. And although it had a suitable ambiance for many boomer churches, it seemed too institutional for the disshelved young people who milled around outside.

Not surprising, many of the usual organic elements were

missing. Though there was low lighting and a free meal served beforehand, the customary candles, interactive stations, and art projects were missing. "It's the product of our environment. It's teaching us the importance of space," stated Mike.

The Rhythm of Discipleship and the Word

Paralleling other organic churches, a missional attitude and small groups proliferate. Small group offerings include courses on spiritual disciplines and theology. Here again, Scum of the Earth parallels many organic congregations, reminding attendees of the necessity to engage hard-core philosophies by stressing that congregants understand theology.

Inspired Rhythms

Inspired Rhythms of Place

Their name creates an image, a sort of cerebral rhythm of place. And Scum of the Earth Church is undoubtedly one of the most original and controversial names I have encountered. But, as I came to know this organic congregation, I saw the name not so much an affront to boomer sensibilities, but a missional decision to help the church bond with the disenfranchised and estranged people it seeks to reach.

"The name resulted from the people we were reaching," stated Mike Sares. "We asked them to choose a name. Reese Roper from the band Five Iron Frenzy suggested Scum of the Earth. I was freaked out and asked everyone to pray about it for a week. In the interim, I called some mentors who told me not to do it.

"Next week we voted, and Scum won. And I'm glad we adopted it. It says a number of things:

—"It says that we don't think too highly of ourselves or act haughtily. This is an impression many people have of Christians. This lets unchurched people know we understand how we are perceived.

—"It says we have humor. People we're reaching like the fact it's an inside joke. Again, it lets them know we are candid and frank people.

—"And, it says we understand they feel rejected by society and even the church."

Scum of the Earth helps people understand that Jesus sees them for who they are, with value and worth. And the scriptural basis for their name reminds them that animosity must be met with love, for Paul described the apostolic life: "To this very hour we go hungry and thirsty, we are in rags, we are brutally treated, we are homeless. We work hard with our own hands. When we are cursed, we bless; when we are persecuted, we endure it; when we are slandered, we answer kindly. Up to this moment we have become the scum of the earth, the refuse of the world" (1 Corinthians 4:11-13).

Inspired Rhythms of Worship

Worship is led by a plurality of leaders, but the night I attended, Deva Yoder led worship. Although female worship leaders should be common in congregations, in my travels through the organic church, male worship leaders have dominated. And although this might be due to the timing of my visit, it does require a word of caution. Allowing women to participate fully in all areas of leadership including worship is in this writer's eyes a hallmark of God-infused ministry.

Thus, female leadership in worship was a welcome break from my customary experience. I found the melodic, pleasant-sounding, and engaging female voice a refreshing worship facet. This use of women in the church is something the church as a whole must carefully cultivate and nurture. It should do so not only for effectiveness, but also because the equality of God's intentions requires it.

An Interview with My Tour Guides

Mike Sares and Eric Bain (*copastors*)

You say experience has led you to see the importance of space. What do you mean?
Eric: We learned this due to our facilities. The Toll Gate was located on Colfax Street, a tough part of town. And the roughest part of the crowd wanted to smoke, so they congregated on the stairs leading up to the auditorium. They were very tattooed, very pierced, with really wild hair. When new people came, they had to walk through this gauntlet of tough-looking people. It let people know you're accepted here regardless of what you look like. The Toll Gate's auditorium made the same statement. It looked like a punk version of the Brady Bunch's living room, filled with abstract art, broken lamps, torn couches, and so on. It felt like a struggling artist's studio. Therefore, struggling urban artists felt at home.

People came for more than the ambiance, didn't they?
Eric: Yes. People came for two reasons. One, they were seeking to know Jesus. And two, it was so contradictory to normal church. Many of these people were ostracized in their parents' churches because of their piercings, hairstyles, or tattoos. The Toll Gate space connected with them. It was disheveled, messy, like them. But it was also real, like them.

A church is more than a facility, it's a community. So how does the significance of space factor into this?
Eric: We're always taught that the church isn't a building, but people. But we've been hearing that the Church in the City facility doesn't reflect our people. Remember, this seems too much like their parents' church, and many of them didn't feel accepted there.
Mike: That's why we say we are a church for the left out and for the right brain.

What do you mean?
Eric: Most of the people who come here are very artistic. If

they are Gothic, that is because they are trying to express themselves through how they dress. All sorts of artists come here. And
artists tend to use their dress, tattoos, and piercings as another
kind of pallette.

Mike: By right-brained we mean we want to reach people who
are artistically oriented. We're a church for urban artists to fit in
regardless of the pallette they are experimenting upon.

Eric: But in many churches this has sort of flipped over. Most
churches emphasize the left brain, the analytical side. We focus on
sharing the good news with people of the right-brain, creative
side.

Mike: On the contrary, it's hard to find somebody to fix your
plumbing.

Three Lessons to Consider

Lesson 1

Recognize that your space can shape you. Winston
Churchill once intoned, "We shape our buildings, thereafter they
shape us." [2] As a church growth consultant, I have witnessed a
building's uncanny sway over a congregation's future. And
unfortunately, the long-term and growth suitability of a facility
are usually not sufficiently studied or analyzed. More often cost
per foot, aesthetics, comfort, conformity with other church
designs, and historical expectations result in facilities that can
stunt a church's growth. Here are some brief guidelines for
facility expansion:[3]

(1) *Chose a space in the midst of your mission field.* This
seems obvious, but oftentimes churches choose locations that
are convenient for the staff and not necessarily strategically
located near their mission field. For example, one church
relocated from a central community auditorium to a facility
in a suburban area adjacent to a new elementary school to
which many staff members sent their children. The church
had engendered a reputation for reaching blue-collar residents of the city, but in hindsight, it became evident the afflu-

ence and influence of the staff, and not the mission field, had lead to this locale. As a result, growth waned. Thus, a church's location should be determined not by money or influence, but by where it best serves its mission field. To facilitate this, church leaders must stay engaged and in proximity with the people they serve.

(2) *Ensure that your facility is flexible.* Logic and experience suggest that a church that offers multiple worship styles can concurrently reach several generations and subcultures.[4] And facilities with immovable walls, auditoriums with one configuration, land-locked locales, and poor traffic flow can hinder the development of a multigenerational church. Consequently, use architects who build flexible facilities, who design schools, malls, and multi-use office and warehouse complexes. Also, be cautious about employing architects who build primarily churches, since most church facilities are not built because of need for flexibility or innovation, but because of church mergers, downsizing, or forced relocation.[5]

(3) *Don't shackle yourself fiscally to a facility.* Expenses rise sharply with expanded or new facilities. Although architects and builders will often laud the added income and attendance that new facilities will foster, these projections are often overestimated. Request from the architect or builder hard numbers demonstrating sustained growth in facilities he or she has constructed.

Lesson 2

Feed their stomachs before you feed their souls. Scum of the Earth offers a free buffet-style dinner before their worship expressions. In light of Abraham Maslow's hierarchy of needs, this initiative makes sociological sense. Maslow proposed that people progress from more basic needs to higher needs in a pyramidal fashion. His thesis is that people are not interested in having higher needs met if lower, more basic needs are going unmet (see figure 6).

Figure 6. Maslow's Hierarchy of Needs[6]
and Areas of Likely Conversionary Experience

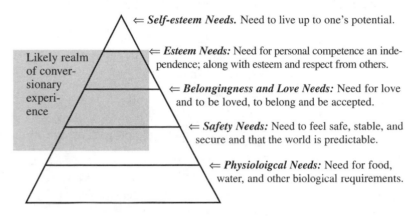

⇐ *Self-esteem Needs.* Need to live up to one's potential.

⇐ *Esteem Needs:* Need for personal competence an independence; along with esteem and respect from others.

⇐ *Belongingness and Love Needs:* Need for love and to be loved, to belong and be accepted.

⇐ *Safety Needs:* Need to feel safe, stable, and secure and that the world is predictable.

⇐ *Physioloigcal Needs:* Need for food, water, and other biological requirements.

Likely realm of conversionary experience

Maslow's hierarchy posits that physiological needs for sustenance (such as food and water) must be met before a person will be interested in the higher needs of "belongingness and love," which might include a conversionary experience or the need to associate with a group of believers. Thus, when we attempt to reach out to the homeless, disenfranchised, or poor without first meeting their physiological (food, shelter) and safety (housing, employment) needs, the growl of an empty stomach or the despair of fiscal calamity may drown out our good news.

Though many churches are engaged in the social mandate,[7] too often this is disconnected from a presentation of the good news. Scum of the Earth does not make this disconnect, instead preceding their worship and teaching expressions with ministries that address attendees' foundational needs.

Lesson 3

Discover if you are called to reach hard- or soft-core post-modernists. The terms *hard-core* and *soft-core,* with reference to postmodernity, have little to do with sexual voyeurism. Rather, these terms are employed by Carl F. H. Henry to differentiate between a more nihilistic sector of postmodern belief and a post-modern worldview that supports ecological, pacifistic, and altruistic concerns.[8] The following is an expanded comparison based on Henry's two distinctions.

Figure 7. A Comparison of Hard-core
and Soft-core Postmodern Views

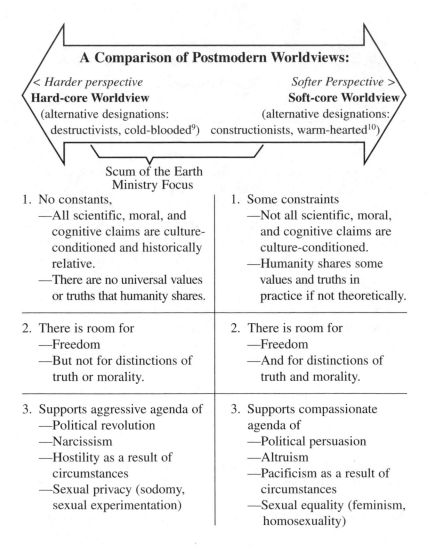

A Comparison of Postmodern Worldviews:

< *Harder perspective* **Hard-core Worldview** (alternative designations: destructivists, cold-blooded[9])	*Softer Perspective* > **Soft-core Worldview** (alternative designations: constructionists, warm-hearted[10])
Scum of the Earth Ministry Focus	
1. No constants, —All scientific, moral, and cognitive claims are culture-conditioned and historically relative. —There are no universal values or truths that humanity shares.	1. Some constraints —Not all scientific, moral, and cognitive claims are culture-conditioned. —Humanity shares some values and truths in practice if not theoretically.
2. There is room for —Freedom —But not for distinctions of truth or morality.	2. There is room for —Freedom —And for distinctions of truth and morality.
3. Supports aggressive agenda of —Political revolution —Narcissism —Hostility as a result of circumstances —Sexual privacy (sodomy, sexual experimentation)	3. Supports compassionate agenda of —Political persuasion —Altruism —Pacificism as a result of circumstances —Sexual equality (feminism, homosexuality)

—Solidarity with libertine standards of living	—Solidarity with impoverished standards of living
4. Subcultures: Goths, skateboarders, disillusioned urbanites, gang members, anarchists.	4. Subcultures: artists, college students, social workers, gay lifestyles, political and social activists.
5. Nihilistic worldview, there is no purpose or meaning.	5. Humanistic worldview, there is purpose and limited meaning.
6. View of history: Boomers have handed down a mess, and alternation is useless.	6. View of history: Boomers have handed down a mess, but alternation is possible.
7. Driving forces —Estrangement —Disconnection —Hopelessness	7. Driving forces —Genuine, albeit flawed community —Connection with altruistic people —Guarded hopefulness

Scum of the Earth has purposely focused its ministry on people who reside in the left of center in figure 7. Though these people require more effort to reach, more patience in discipleship, and more intellectual engagement to penetrate, they are a necessary focus of the church's ministry. George G. Hunter states, "The typical church ignores two populations, year after year: the people who aren't 'refined' enough to feel comfortable with us, and the people who are too 'out of control' for us to feel comfortable with them!"[11]

Few churches are successfully engaged in this difficult endeavor, and more are needed. Thus, ask yourself some of the following questions to ascertain if your ministry is called to engage this intersection of hard-core or soft-core postmodernity.

(1) *Does your faith community include former hard-core post-modernists?* If God has given you a ministry to disenfranchised deconstructionists, then you should observe fruit from this calling. This often means people from this subculture have come to faith in Christ and embarked upon discipleship through your community.

(2) *Does your civic community include hard-core postmodernists?* There is a measure of self-satisfaction that can arise from taking on difficult duties. However, such self-aggrandizing must not lead you to mount a ministry you are not positioned to undertake. Effective ministry to disenfranchised people will be predicated by their presence and upon your willingness to live among them.

If you answered *no* to the above questions, go to Option A. If you answered yes to one or more of the above questions, go to Option B.

Option A. *Hold this mission field lightly.* C. Peter Wagner believes that one lesson from the *Parable of the Soils* (Luke 8:4-15) is that Christians are to sow the knowledge of Christ in the soils (that is, populace) that are the most fertile (that is, receptive).[12] But as we have seen from the comparison of worldviews, the hard-core postmodernist may be more difficult to engage successfully. If this is the case and you are not equipped to reach this constituency, do not abandon them entirely, but in Donald McGavran's terminology, "hold them lightly."[13] By this, McGavran meant to pray for and engage them while being cognizant of any growing receptivity. This includes continuing effective service and altruistic presence among them, but waiting for God's provision or timing to engage them fully. To do so prematurely or ill-equipped may result in failed efforts and even increased estrangement.

Option B. *If you answered* yes *to questions 1 or 2, then begin carefully but purposefully to mount a ministry to hard-core postmodernists.* Study the examples of other churches who are succeeding in this area, such as Scum of the Earth in Denver, The Bridge in Phoenix, or St. Thomas' Church in Sheffield, England (and their urban Forge ministry). In addition, take on the role of a missionary to this culture, learning what anthropologist Paul Hiebert calls their "integrated system of learned patterns of behavior, ideas and products,"[14] and which "includes not only language, but all symbol systems" such as the use of time, space, gestures, and rituals.[15] Only after a comprehensive appraisal, penetration, and awareness of their culture will you be ready to engage them.

CHAPTER 10

Bluer
Minneapolis, Minnesota

Seven out of ten adults (71 percent) say they have never experienced God's presence at a church service.
—*George Barna, pollster and author*[1]

First Encounters

Googling "bluer" and "Minneapolis," I was surprised when my browser window said, "Bluer: The Minneapolis Vineyard Church." I had heard good things about this emerging organic church, but I did not suspect a Vineyard connection.

Vineyard is a movement of Charismatic churches[2] that formed an association under the guidance of church growth consultant and author John Wimber. Since their inception, Vineyard churches have remained largely boomer congregations with a few exceptions. Therefore, I was pleasantly surprised to find that Bluer was a Vineyard outreach to postmodern young people.

"We used to be North Metro Vineyard," began John Musick, who now shepherds this congregation. "In fact, we were the youth and college ministry, but we kind of packaged the good news. Now we experience it. And this transition happened because we embrace the provisional nature of God, looking for him to provide 'miracle' facilities. And he did!"

Dashboard

Church: Bluer (formerly North Metro Vineyard Church)
Leaders: John Musick (pastor), Dan Lukas (worship leader)
Location: South Minneapolis, Minnesota, in the facilities of another organic congregation, Solomon's Porch
Affiliation: Association of Vineyard Churches USA
Size: 125 +
Audience: People in their twenties to mid-forties, artists, college students, graduate students, metropolitan residents, service industry workers
Websites: www.emerginggod.com; www.creativechurch.org; www.bluer.org

A Fusion of Rhythms

Shared Rhythms

The Rhythm of Place

The worship space of Bluer was inviting and comfortable but looked strangely familiar. I found the venue reminiscent of pictures I had seen of another organic congregation, Solomon's Porch. It turned out that Solomon's Porch (profiled in chapter 12) had allowed Bluer to use its worship space on Saturday nights. This communal and flexible arrangement was attractive to the Bluer congregation.

Lit primarily with candles, the worship space was filled with over a dozen couches and five times as many easy chairs. The room was arranged in a square, and the focus was thus toward a central space where two stools sat. Off to one side, a worship team was positioned away from the center of attention. This comfortable ambiance and coziness lulled me into a peaceful yet anticipatory mood. And by limiting distractions, it allowed me to focus upon my encounter with Jesus, not upon the preparation of the musicians. While visiting boomer churches, I often experience a somewhat institutional, if not sterile milieu. But here I felt as if I were back in a friend's home, amid the casual comfort of those who loved and cared.

The Rhythm of Worship

Worship followed a somewhat usual Vineyard structure, with thirty to forty-five minutes of worship, followed by a thirty-minute sermon and a time of prayer.

However, the music departed from my Vineyard expectations, for the Vineyard Movement is known for music that melds together joyful songs with catchy country-rock arrangements. John Wimber himself had been a musician and songwriter. Subsequently, musical staples birthed in the Vineyard Movement can be heard in boomer congregations of all denominational affiliations, but regrettably with somewhat generic arrangements. However, at Bluer, these Vineyard songs were given a fresh and techno-savvy reinterpretation. The updated rhythm, accompanied by plain, almost spoken vocalizations, rendered a gritty yet authentic rendition.

I knew John Wimber while we were both involved at Fuller Seminary. John shaped his charismatic view of the validity of the gifts of the Holy Spirit from his exegesis of Scripture and his logical assessment. With Wimber, experience followed logical analysis. Analyze Scripture, see the validity of the gifts of the Holy Spirit, then experience them in the logical setting of a worship gathering (which at Fuller Seminary Wimber glibly called "laboratories"). In other words, for Wimber, analysis and intellect brought along his emotions. It was this acceptance of the more remarkable gifts of the Holy Spirit, based upon a logical understanding of God's Word, that attracted many people to the Vineyard Movement. These churches offered places where being emotional was not just enjoyable, but logical too.

What is interesting is that Bluer is reacting to Wimber's logical approach and instead is underscoring an experiential element. Subsequently, those at Bluer seek the mystical and authentic aspects of an encounter with Jesus. Thus, their music sought to be conducive to this spiritual intersection. Though the songs were familiar, the musical arrangements allowed extended periods of instrumental music. Filled with a sweeping fusion of electronic sounds, sometimes reminiscent of the seashore, other times of a storm, the beauty of the music allowed the listener to be propelled into spiritual encounter. Not unlike the pictorial musical passages of Antonio Vivaldi's *The Four Seasons,* Bluer's unhurried progress and musical vistas allowed the music to become secondary to the condition of my heart. A lush and orchestrated styling afforded these familiar songs new power and impact as they softly but slowly led me from my comfortable easy chair into the presence of my Lord.

The Rhythm of Discipleship and the Word

Here Bluer followed closely Vineyard theology and practice. Bluer also offers a vibrant prayer ministry, as well as outreach to the urban community. In addition, small groups (a Vineyard hallmark) proliferate throughout the congregation, including "Bluer Man Group," a men's accountability group, and "Going Deeper," a group probing the depths of discipleship and interdependence.

It was the idea of "going deeper" that gave rise to the name Bluer. In their personality statement they state, "The name 'bluer' comes from our desire to be authentic and genuine; truer than true blue: bluer. We feel the world is looking for something real and that we are never more real than when we are connected with our creator in authentic communion with Him and with other followers of Jesus." [3]

James D. G. Dunn, in his comprehensive study *Jesus and the Spirit,* describes Paul's viewpoint as, "He recognizes that God and his Spirit may be experienced in many diverse ways, both in non-rational ecstasy and through the mind, but in experiences of dramatically effective power and in compulsion to serve, both in inspiration to pray and praise and in inspiration to preach and teach." [4] This would also be a good description of what I experienced on my travels with Bluer.

Inspired Rhythms

Inspired Rhythms of Place

A distinguishing characteristic is Bluer's "endeavor to embrace the provisional nature of God by looking for 'miracle' facilities." [5]

Birthed in the struggles of North Metro Vineyard's search for permanent and suitable facilities, this youth-orientated offspring adopted facility flexibility as a strategic trait.

North Metro Vineyard was fourteen years old when John Musick took over the church's young adult ministry named Bluer, which had passed the 125-150 people in attendance at North Metro Vineyard Church. And each week both North Metro Vineyard and Bluer produced large worship events. Bluer used over $20,000 of audio equipment, professional musicians, and elaborate stage lighting. North Metro Vineyard had a similar extensive setup of musicians and worship leaders. "In the church world it was a success," recalled Musick. "But we also sensed a growing insincerity. The production came before purpose."

The size of these worship productions necessitated a theatrical-style venue. Due to the difficulty in regularly renting such facilities, North Metro Vineyard and Bluer eventually united into one congregation with one worship celebration. Bluer was now adopted as the name of the united congregation.

But Bluer's large weekly production still suffered through numerous facility transitions. Eventually, when forced to leave a theatre they had thought would be a permanent home, the church leaders discovered that the only venue available was Solomon's Porch, which resembled a large living room.

Solomon's Porch's laid-back and peaceful environment was a respite for many of the harried Bluer leaders. Though some felt called to large-scale worship events and left for other churches, many Bluer leaders were on the verge of burnout and found the organic church a refreshing new way to connect to God. "I didn't think there was anything wrong with a big worship production," recalled John Musick, "but we came back each night tired and burned out." Eventually the environs of Solomon's Porch had an effect on Bluer, for many found they preferred the heightened intimacy and decreased exhaustion of an organic gathering, and soon they began to bring their friends.

An Interview with My Tour Guide

John Musick (*pastor*)

You are dealing with a delicate subject: preference in worship styles. And you've warned about the potential for insincerity in worship due to an emphasis on performance and professionalism. But you've been on both sides.

You're right. At Bluer, we used to do all the big, lavish worship production stuff. We did everything but shoot me out of a cannon. Our problem with this performance type of worship was that the results were very unsettling. People were not connecting. They just watched and left. There was no small group incorporation, no transformation, no community.

What do you think caused this?

We asked those who attended and found that the majority were from other churches. Bluer was supposed to connect unchurched people to God. But we were just connecting existing Christians. There is nothing wrong with that. Christians need to connect with God. But that wasn't our mission. There were already plenty of churches out there connecting churched people with Jesus. I guess Vineyards were founded on Wimber's ideas about church growth and that you reach people who don't know Jesus. We weren't, and it was humbling.

And the change came about when you had no place to go but to Solomon's Porch?

Right! When Bluer began to share church space with Solomon's Porch we were forced to engage one another because it was in the round. No longer did we have the fancy lights and all the gizmos and gadgets. It was just us. We had to get to know one another. Then we found that this kind of laid-back environment revived us. Plus, we discovered that it was not only attractive to unchurched people, but also helped us connect better with them.

Any regrets?

No, it was a journey, and I've changed. My style of communicating changed from being a speaker and entertainer to being a fellow sojourner. Even though it was humbling, I wouldn't trade it for anything in the world, for it brought us to where we are now. Church shouldn't be a destination, but a vehicle by which people experience God.

Three Lessons to Consider

Lesson 1

Marginalized churches can grow into organic congregations. Churches that are marginalized due to the age of congregants and worship styles can morph into organic congregations in which flexibility, adaptability, and spiritual encounter are more attainable. The following are seven steps that can accomplish this transition:

(1) *Ask yourself, is hosting multiple worship expressions preferable?* If so, go to 1.a. If not, go to 1.b.

(a) Sometimes hosting multiple worship styles for multiple generations is preferable. This is especially attractive if there are two or more generations within the church already. If this course is chosen, a seven-step process for building a Multi-gen. church can be found in my book, *A House Divided: Bridging the Generation Gaps in Your Church.*[6] However, in Bluer's case, the size of the church, lack of venues, and impending burnout of leaders meant that hosting multiple worship styles with full-scale worship productions was no longer appealing. In such circumstances, go to 1.b.

(b) If growing a multi-generational church is not possible, then an option may be to transform into an organic congregation. In Bluer's case, the sons and daughters of many North Metro Vineyard attendees were gaining responsibility in worship, evangelism, and church ministries. This increasing involvement of Generation X gave them a taste for leadership. As such, they desired to make over the church in a more authentic and less hectic entity. Once they experienced the intimate and authentic environ of Solomon's Porch, there was no going back. Subsequently, if you have a smaller, stagnant, or declining boomer congregation, the handing of the reins to a younger generation may allow the church to morph into a more authentic and calming organic personality.

(2) *Decide if you have sufficient mass (thirty-five-plus) for the metamorphosis process.* Consider the size of the Generation X subcongregation. If it is fewer than thirty-five, it will have difficulty attracting the minimum number of attendees needed to survive. Usually thirty-five-plus provides enough people at worship gatherings for a measure of autonomy, yet kinship. Smaller worship gatherings are often too personal for newcomers to feel at ease. However, if a Generation X contingent in your church has or can quickly absorb others to reach this number, then progress to step 3.

(3) *Bathe every strategic plan and every leader with prayer.* Prayer is the one indispensable step in the process. Prayers for leaders as well as for strategies must become an integral and regular part of the planning process.[7] Thus, prayer becomes a foundational priority. Eddie Gibbs points out that "as one studies case histories of growing churches, there is one recurring factor—they are all *praying* churches."[8]

(4) *Begin to mentor younger generations in the mechanics and expectations of leadership.* Employ a mentorship model to allow younger generations to experience the regimens of church leadership in assistant roles before they take the reins. But do not expect them wholly to adopt your management style or methods. Although acceptance of the biblical message is expected, acceptance of methodology is not. Let them indigenize and customize your leadership practices. Also allow a degree of floundering and uncertainty as they learn through experience.

(5) *Set a date and a location for the end of one church and the birth of a new and organic congregation.* Designate a point at which to transfer leadership to the younger generation.

Boomers should resist the temptation to continue the mentoring process indefinitely. Boomers must fully and completely pass the baton. Few things are more disastrous than when the runner handing off the baton refuses to relinquish his or her grasp, causing the ensuing runner to falter.

(6) *Allow collegiate rather than paternal accountability.* Allow denominational leadership and, if an independent congregation, interdenominational colleagues to provide accountability rather than the church's former boomer leadership. Accountability by spiritually mature colleagues is preferable at this stage than paternal leadership. Former boomer leaders are often conveniently at hand and are anxious to offer advice, but the paternal nature of such advice will carry too much baggage. Allow transdenominational networks or informal collegiate networks to provide advice and counsel, rather than paternal admonitions.

(7) *Employ evaluation tools to ensure that new directions actually move you forward.* Though young people are brimming with new ideas, they may have been raised in a church in which boomer management practices, such as lack of evaluation, have plateaued attendance. Thus, without an ongoing and planned evaluation process, the organic church may inadvertently adopt some of the practices of its progenitors and then plateau. The key to preventing plateau is innovation, coupled with evaluation. Also ensure that evaluation is holistic and not just focused on numbers. According to Acts 2:42-47, biblical church growth measures four types of church growth: (a) maturing in faith, prayer, and discipleship; (b) growing in unity; (c) meeting community needs and benefiting from community favor; and (d) finally growing in numbers. Field-tested tools for measuring these four types of growth are available in my earlier books.[9]

Lesson 2

Be careful not to allow an attachment to place or style to affect flexibility, innovation, and perhaps evangelical effectiveness. As we saw with North Metro Vineyard and Bluer, holding large worship events limited their flexibility, damaged their volunteer base, and decreased effectiveness. However, at the genesis of their movement, Vineyard churches avoided the customary church facility, choosing instead innovative spaces such as warehouses, shopping centers, grocery stores, and the like. Subsequently, these large facilities allowed Vineyard to host expansive worship gatherings. However, over time, this innovation became tradition. And the large inflexible production lost much of its effectiveness for reaching unchurched young people.

Bluer reminds us that a subtle dependence and identity can become attached to the styles and places we employ, regardless of their flexibility. Effectiveness in reaching a community is often tied to innovation and flexibility, something that too often wanes as a congregation and its traditions grow. The story of Bluer's eschewing of North Metro Vineyard's large facilities and large productions demonstrates that organic churches can often blossom from marginalized congregations.

Lesson 3

Allow musical passages to paint mental pictures and thus usher you into spiritual encounter. Music can entertain and divert us with lighthearted froth and merriment. But it can also paint a musical image that allows reflection and meditation. It is this later contemplative and reflective element that is often lacking in boomer churches.

The power of a spiritual encounter is preserved at Bluer by reinterpreting classic Vineyard worship songs with a more extended and elaborate musical ornamentation that sweeps the listener from his or her seat into an encounter with God. While celebratory adulation to our God is expected, so is contemplative and pensive reflection, for as Asaph the psalmist intoned, "I remembered my songs in the night. My heart mused and my spirit inquired" (Psalm 77:6).

CHAPTER 11

Tribe of Los Angeles
Los Angeles, California

Everything is to sound like radio, like the echo of mass culture in all its might.

—Theodor W. Adorno, sociologist and author[1]

First Encounters

As I departed Tribe of Los Angeles, I carried with me an abstract but poignant painting I had completed during the sermon. To most observers, it might appear as an ill-defined ship in the midst of a dark blue field, but to me, it represented a spiritual journey. That night, I spent nearly twenty minutes in personal reflection and prayer and then was guided to express my fears of loneliness in paint. As I departed, I left with a sense I had encountered some of my own insecurities, and they had been swept away by an awareness of God's companionship. It was welcomed and needed.

"That's a good painting," offered a young man that my wife Rebecca and I had met at the Tribe. He was gracious artistically but accurate spiritually.

Dashboard

Church: Tribe of Los Angeles
Leaders: Rebecca Ver Straten-McSparran (pastor), David Raven (worship facilitator)

Location: 5828 Wilshire Boulevard, Los Angeles, California
Affiliations: The National Association of Congregational
   Christian Churches
Size: 25-55
Audience: People in their twenties to late forties, urban artists,
   seminary students, metropolitan residents, and entertainment
   industry workers
Website: www.tribela.com

A Fusion of Rhythms

Shared Rhythms

The Rhythm of Place

A few weeks after I visited, the Tribe moved to Wilshire
Boulevard, across from The Screen Actors Guild and the L.A.
County Museum of Art. "It really helps us reach out to people in
the entertainment industry who live in the area," reflected Ver
Straten-McSparran, who is also director of the Los Angeles Film
Study Center.

Inspired Rhythms

Inspired Rhythms of Worship

"Our worship expression is designed around the drumming circle," stated Ver Straten-McSparran. Drumming circles appeal to
generations raised on a proliferation of rhythmic music. The
rhythmic format of a drumming circle will be examined in the following chapter, but for this present discussion we will look at how
they are organized.

   Attendees sit in an ever-widening circle, facing inward, and
each person is provided a percussive instrument. Instruments
include African drums, maracas, djembes, congas, dumbeks,
handmade shakers, bongos, scrapers, tambourines, and bells.
Chant-like singing accompanies the drumming. To add an

aspect of musical tone, a "groove-box," a prerecorded CD of synthesizer-created mood music, is used. Similar to the music at Bluer, but more freeform and without a melody, the groove-box gives tonal structure, but not too much, to the rhythms of the worship. Such organic and raw drumming rails against what sociologist Theodor Adorno calls the "echo of mass culture," in which "predigested . . . baby food" describes most music.[2]

Though the worship expression is elastic, the following is the general structure:

A **meal** open to all begins the evening.

The **light of Christ** is brought in to light a candle on the altar.

Reflection. Attendees are allowed to meditate on Scripture or a reflective passage for ten to twenty minutes. "People today aren't accustomed to spending this much time in prayer and reflection," stated Ver Straten-McSparran. "But this prepares them to listen to what God is saying." The evening I attended, the following reflective passage from The Heidelberg Catechism was used:

> *What is your only comfort in life and in death?*
> *That I am not my own,*
> *But belong—*
> *Body and soul,*
> *In life and in death—*
> *To my faithful Savior Jesus Christ.*

Drumming and chanting.[3] This may not be for everyone, including for my former seminary professor who asked with a wink and a nod, "Did you do some drumming?" But for many young people raised on the rhythmic underpinnings of "world music," this is a fresh and relevant way to worship.

A **sermon** with audience participation followed.

The worship concluded with **the Eucharist, the Lord's Prayer,** and a **benediction**.

Inspired Rhythms of Discipleship and the Word

Sermons at the Tribe excel at providing a generous dose of give-and-take, with questions, comments, discussion, and even criticism. Critique and appraisal are permitted not to foster confusion, but to allow the listener to think logically through the implications of the world we live in and biblical explanations. Thus, the listener is allowed to "connect the dots" and participate in the deduction of a biblical conclusion.

Autumn Fiore, a Fuller Seminary–trained psychologist, delivered a sermon using artistic interactivity to emphasize that God is the answer to our estrangement and loneliness. It began with scriptures that never mentioned God, but rather demonstrated an understanding of loneliness and isolation. We were given paints and paper and were instructed to portray our reactions to these scriptures. My drawing began murky and dark. Slowly, but deliberately, Fiore added scriptures that illuminated humankind's need for companionship and community. Over the next half hour, scriptures brought us slowly but logically to the conclusion that God sees our estrangement and loneliness and has provided his Holy Spirit as a comforter and answer.

An Interview with My Tour Guide

Rebecca Ver Straten-McSparran (*pastor*)

How did Tribe of Los Angeles come about?

I was a pastor in a congregational church, but my husband and I wanted to reach out to people like us, to those who wanted to worship more "wholly" with contemplative and natural elements. We've attended Burning Man celebration in the Nevada desert, where thousands of people gather to create a giant sculpture. It's sort of a postmodern gathering of free souls. We weren't there to reach a particular group of people, which is what some people do. That creates inauthentic relationships. Rather, reaching out should grow naturally out of the people who are creating the ministry. Only then will it be authentic, reaching those with similar desires. Because participatory percussion is a big part of our lives, as well as is Burning Man, we used percussion to welcome people into a worship expression. And we did, but we also reached a lot of seminary students and Christians who wanted a reflective and engaging way to worship. We've had to adjust to reaching both crowds.

Describe a drum circle.

Our entire worship involves a drum circle. We generally have no guitar, no keyboard; only percussion instruments and a groovebox. Songs are almost chanted. There are plenty of drums, so everyone can join in. The congregation thus creates worship. Everybody is involved; there are no watchers. Many churches have a band leading. But we are organic, helping the entire congregation participate. This is very much based on our understanding of the priesthood of believers.

How do you foster interactivity in sermons?

The key is a lot of preparation and prayer. I have used art projects in my sermons, such as paints, clay, and so on. I include talking points and questions in my sermons and sometimes put questions up on a screen and ask everyone to break into groups or individually to write about what it means to them. Its helps us connect to people and then connect them to the Holy Spirit.

Three Lessons to Consider

Lesson 1

Develop interactivity in sermons. While analyzing Vintage Faith and One Place, I saw how they used interactivity to enhance worship segments or substitute for sermons. Neither church limited interactivity to the worship segment, but also used it during sermons. However, the Tribe embraces interactivity as an essential component of all sermonizing to better communicate spiritual truths. This is an approach to truth delivery that needs to be emphasized to better reach younger generations raised upon technological interactivity, including video games, movies on demand, text-messaging, and the Internet.

Rebecca Ver Straten-McSparran carefully builds this into every sermon, resulting in art projects, interactive stations, journaling, discussion, small group involvement, role-play, questions, and video/film segments.[4] The idea is to foster physical action and mental reflection on behalf of the listener and to better investigate and inculcate the ideas being discussed.

Lesson 2

Use natural theology, in addition to revealed theology, to allow scriptural truth to become logically evident. Sermons at the Tribe's gatherings allow listeners to employ their own mental faculties to the evidence presented and then to "connect the dots." This approach is sometimes called moving from "natural theology" to "revealed theology" and will be needed to reach out to unchurched people who have been exposed to varied religious systems and who have little interest in or respect for Christianity.

Revealed theology, on the one hand, can be defined as knowledge of God (that is, theology) that has been "revealed" to us through special revelation, such as the Bible, the Holy Spirit, the Church, doctrine, or another Christian. Natural theology, on the other hand, occurs when a person is permitted to think through the evidence about God with his or her "natural" intellect, connect the dots himself or herself, and induce a conclusion.[5]

For example, revealed theology occurs when a preacher says, "God created the heavens and the earth," with an indirect command that the listener either accept or reject this. The biblical principle is stated, and the listener is expected to accept or reject it by faith. Logical validation is not explored, or if so, only barely. The statement's source, the Bible, and, thus ultimately, God are held forth as the validation of this claim, and the listener should accept it because of its source. Faith is thus the required (and appropriate) response.

Now, let me say in the strongest terms there is nothing wrong with revealed theology and requisite faith. In fact, both are needed to help us comprehend God's plan for humankind's salvation. Most sermonizing is and should be revealed theology, eliciting a faith response. But, it is sometimes helpful to build a foundation through reason (the natural intellect and natural theology) for the principles that will ultimately need to be accepted by faith (that is, through revealed theology).

This is precisely what the Tribe's sermon accomplished. The first part of the sermon explored the unhealthy effects of loneliness, then progressed to how loneliness creates estrangement. Next, the need for a friend who will not abandon us was deduced. All this was accomplished through logical induction and natural theology.

But then the sermon turned to revealed theology, demonstrating that God had provided an avenue through his Son and his Holy Spirit to provide that friendship. Thus, the sermon started with a foundation of rational deduction (natural theology) and worked its way to presenting the biblical answer (revealed theology).

To jaded and antagonistic unchurched people, an appeal to the natural intellect is often necessary to legitimize and commence communication.[6] They are not convinced by our proof texts or by our pronouncements that "we've always done it that way" (both revealed theology). But there is a caveat. This approach requires more preparation, research, and assessment. However, if the truth in Scripture is valid, as this author believes it is, then allowing the listener to apply cogent logic and analysis to humanity's plight and biblical answers may be the best way to reach reticent hearers.

To contrast the influence and efficacy of revealed and natural theology upon sermon styles, I have created figure 8.

Figure 8. Preaching Typology in Traditional, Contemporary, and Organic Milieus

Sermon Styles	Sermon Traits	Truth[7] delivery principles	Ambiance and mood created	Who it primarily reaches
Traditional Preaching (dominant style up to the 1950s)	—Sermons laden with slogans, catchphrases, and mottos. —Lessons in sermons may be unclear, but emphasis that "Jesus is Lord" is evident and retainable.	*Revealed Theology:* I unite with a community and rally around the Truth as revealed.	—Come prepared to rally/rejoice around God's principles —An emotional and social event (e.g., revival) —Spiritual deductions often grow out of the emotional nature of the event.	—*Churched people,* many of whom may be marginalized Christians in need of an enthusiastic and communal boost to their faith.
Contemporary Preaching	—Lessons and teaching are employed —Three-point	*Revealed Theology:* The Truth is taught to me.	—Come prepared to rally around God's lessons for life.	—*Churched people* but also some *unchurched people* who are biblically

(dominant style from the 1960s to the 1980s)	lessons in sermons are clear, with high "take-home value," emphasizing the personal benefit of Jesus' teachings.		—An intellectual teaching event, with emotional aspects (e.g., seminar/lecture with worship). —Spiritual deductions grow out of the applicability of the principles studied.	illiterate, but who hunger for knowledge and understanding.
Organic Preaching (1990s to today in organic churches)	—Questioning, dialogue, and argumentation is encouraged. —Lessons in sermons are logically supportable when the listener thinks them through.	*Natural Theology:* I conclude the Truth is logical, that is, I think through and rationally infer the validity of biblical Truth.	—Come prepared to think through what you hear and rally around the logic and validity of God's principles. —Spiritual deductions grow out of logical inductions.	—*Unchurched people* who have been exposed to many religious systems, and who have little initial interest in or respect for Christianity.

Lesson 3

Live among the people you serve. Oftentimes as a church grows, Christians will unconsciously distance themselves emotionally and physically from the people they serve. Donald McGavran labeled this malady "redemption and lift," for as a person embarks upon a life redeemed by Christ, one naturally behaves in a way that removes him or her from the everyday life of people who do not yet know Christ.[8] There is a positive aspect to lift, for a person is raised above the morass of former immoral behavior. But there is also a caveat, for a person has less in common emotionally and socially with acquaintances that he or she seeks to reach. Thus, evangelism often wanes, as lift occurs.

One solution is to stay deliberately connected with the people you serve.[9] This does not mean participating in immorality, but rather living in proximity and interaction, so that your understanding of their milieu remains intact. The Tribe embraces this ethos. Rebecca Ver Straten-McSparran has helped move the film school she leads to the area. "We have fifty students living in the area. And I'm the religious representative on several area art boards, including some in Hollywood. We're ministering to a lot of the entertainment industry by being in proximity. And people in the Tribe are increasingly moving into the neighborhood. It's a good thing." I would agree.

CHAPTER 12

Solomon's Porch
Minneapolis, Minnesota

Recycling is no longer confined to diet coke cans and Evian water bottles. It's become one of the dominant impulses in American culture today. . . . Whether you call it nostalgia, postmodernism or a simple vandalizing of the past, all this recycling essentially amounts to the same thing: a self-conscious repudiation of originality.

—*Michiko Kakutani, journalist and winner of the Pulitzer Prize for Criticism*[1]

First Encounters

Though Mars Hill and St. Tom's are two of the largest organic churches I visited, Solomon's Porch may be one of the most influential, having been featured in the *Wall Street Journal,* the *New York Times,* and *Time* magazine. And though mid-sized, Solomon's Porch embraces an improvisational artistry that the mainstream media recognizes as influential beyond its size.

This influence affected me when at the end of the worship gathering I stated to Al, "That was the quickest hour and a half I can remember."

"Where did the time go?" came Al's bewildered reply. Al is the pastor of a large boomer congregation in Minneapolis, as well as one of my students in the College of Graduate Studies at Indiana Wesleyan University. Later as we recalled the evening, we acknowledged that creativity, imagination, inventiveness, and ingenuity had kept this evening from becoming dull or boring.

Solomon's Porch is known as a congregation that embraces innovation and experimentation to keep worship from becoming stale, prefabricated, or disengaged. Doug Pagitt, the shepherd, once stated, "Our worship gatherings almost feel like great improv—the band plays from memory, not from sheet music, and the sermon is created as it comes, not read from a written text. Someone may spontaneously share a brand-new poem or song. Communion is introduced by a different person each week, and there's no set script. Post-sermon discussions are free-form conversations with no agenda but to stay reasonably close to the subject at hand." [2]

This is a church full of creativity and subsequent surprises. Surprises occurred not only at the end of the evening but also at the beginning, for though this was Memorial Day weekend, Solomon's Porch was packed. To add to my puzzlement, the weather this Sunday evening was beautiful and this was Minnesota, where summer notoriously arrives late.

Now to be candid, I am frequently bored during my visits to nonorganic churches. It is not that I am disinterested in spiritual matters, for I have a deep passion and interest in serving and worshiping my Lord Jesus. But I often find that poor execution and uninspiring traditions rob me of engagement. I find my mind unintentionally wandering away from my Lord and onto mundane things. Not because I want to, but because the worship experience has become predictable, prefabricated, and disengaging.[3]

No such experience greeted me at Solomon's Porch. I found myself in a genuine spiritual encounter with God. It was refreshing, revitalizing, and it was welcomed.

Dashboard

Church: Solomon's Porch

Leaders: Doug Pagitt (pastor), Ben Johnson (director of music), Tom Karki (church administrator), Abby Andrusko (director of Vecinos)

Location: South Minneapolis, Minnesota

Affiliation: Evangelical Covenant Church

Size: 250+

Audience: Primarily people in their twenties through mid-forties, artists, college students, graduate students, metropolitan residents, service industry workers, college/postmodern thinkers, multiple generations

Website: www.solomonsporch.com

A Fusion of Rhythms

Shared Rhythms

The Rhythm of Place

The auditorium at Solomon's Porch replicates a living room environment, with comfy chairs, soft lighting, coffee tables, and engaging paintings. It creates an environment that fosters casualness and interaction among the attendees even before the gathering commences.[4]

The auditorium is on the second floor and, like some other organic congregations, is set with the stage in the center and seating facing inward. Solomon's Porch does this to get away from a "front-facing, stage-focused approach,"[5] which Pagitt points out originated in the 1880s as a theatre metaphor and evolved in the 1960s into the "concert setting, which hung onto the stage-focused environment with performers on one level and the audience on another."[6] Solomon's Porch desires to avoid this distinction between performer and participant.

The Rhythm of Worship

Songs were imbued with a gritty, realistic, and humble tenor. They were engaging and decidedly Christian. Often based word-for-word upon Scripture, they were accompanied by a melodic but not overly orchestrated arrangement.

Historical and liturgical elements were also integrated during the invocation, confessional, and prayers. This amalgamation of rituals alongside modern expressions helps participants connect with both their historical roots as well as modern cultural expressions.

The Rhythm of Discipleship and the Word

Solomon's Porch mirrors many organic churches with an outreach to its urban neighbors. However, they do not see themselves as the only entity involved in this endeavor, but rather team players with other churches and social service agencies. For their contribution, Solomon's Porch created "vecinos," the Spanish word for neighbor. Language classes, a mentoring and tutoring program, community meals, after-school activities, and a food and clothing shelf help the church engage its neighbors. Vecinos director Abby Andrusko states, "It is because of the gospel of Jesus that we find reason to share life and serve those closest to us not only relationally . . . but proximity-wise as well."

The missional attitude witnessed in many organic congregations is also reflected in this congregation, which describes itself as "a holistic, missional Christian community."[7] Spiritual formation takes place in Bible studies, small groups, art discussions, and Wednesday night dinners.

In addition, the theological content of the sermon is decidedly in congruence with the Evangelical Covenant Church, a denomination with which this congregation is affiliated. Plus, the sermons frequently center around an extended portion of Scripture, often a chapter or two long, and attendees share in the reading. Various translations are sometimes used to give further insight. This integration of biblical context with audience participation allows for heightened engagement and understanding.

Finally, I noticed that Pagitt did not hurry through his presentation. He allowed the Holy Spirit to work though the Christians present. Questions, comments, and repartee were encouraged. This, happily, took the focus off the communicator and onto the content of the communication.

Inspired Rhythms

Inspired Rhythms of Place

At the time of this writing, the worship venue is a converted office building on a side street in South Minneapolis. The first floor holds an Internet cafe and an art gallery where congregational artists display their craft. Some of the artwork spills out into the hallways, where art projects line the hall.

The worship space reminded me of a large living room.[8] Twenty to twenty-five sofas and sixty to seventy chairs, ranging from overstuffed easy chairs to bar stools, filled the room. Artists in the congregation have painted the room in muted shades of purple, with accents of green and gold. In addition, each week the environment evolves as visual artists replace and add colorful fabrics, paintings, and sculptures. Candles, table lamps, and coffee tables complement the environment, creating an inviting, relaxing, and pleasant environ. "Aesthetics—and all that it stirs in us— matters to our community," stated Pagitt.[9]

Solomon's Porch embraces creativity not just for art's sake, but because creativity is a characteristic of our heavenly Father's work and character. Pagitt believes that encouraging these creative juices in God's children helps us indigenize worship to modern cultures.[10] Thus, Pagitt follows Charles Kraft's viewpoint that though Christ is above, he also works through a culture, judging some aspects and accepting other altruistic elements, for the transformation of the whole.[11] Pagitt sees this in art, and not just in the musical arts, but in a variety of artistic expressions including painting, sculpture, mixed-media, and electronic forms. Pagitt would agree with Kraft who stated, "I see cultural structuring, however, as basically a vehicle or milieu, neutral in essence, though warped by the pervasive influences of human sinfulness." Toward that end, Solomon's Porch is sifting and probing cultural predilections to strip off immoral disfigurations and reclaim those artistic and God-given talents that can help artists grow in their Christian maturity and mission. Kraft called this a "venturesome [participation] with God in the transformation of a culture."[12]

Inspired Rhythms of Worship

It might seem contradictory, but to foster creativity and improvisation, a lot of preparation is required. And thus, Sunday evenings at Solomon's Porch are given a general structure, but within that structure there is a lot of room for the Holy Spirit to participate through the talents of the professional and amateur artists involved. First let's look at the musical structure.

On Wednesday evenings, a "musical collaboration" is held in the auditorium. Here, professional as well as amateur musicians are invited to improvise and write music. Out of this often comes musical elements for the weekend's worship gathering. Though songs may be improvised or sketched out in advance, the Wednesday evening collaboration gives the basic direction for the songs as they unfold. The songs are not assigned a final form prior to Sunday, but rather are given general parameters. This is analogous to what Alan Roxburgh calls a "bounded-set" structure rather than a "centered-set" structure.[13] On the one hand, by "centered-set," Roxburgh means a leadership style by which a leader at the center makes the decisions and sets the direction. All participants look to the central leader for direction and cohesiveness. On the other hand, a bounded-set leadership structure means the leadership is less obvious or didactic; but rather there are "bounds" that are "set" within which a lot of improvisation is allowed. Such bounds could be theological, denominational, or aesthetic. It is these bounds that are intuitively worked out on Wednesdays.

The evening I attended, the *lectio divina*[14] was used. While the musicians led in a simple song based on these scriptures, the congregants asked God to reveal what this passage was saying to them personally. Pagitt kept the evening from becoming stale by adding and subtracting the musical accompaniment of the *lectio divina*. Sometimes our biblical contemplations were accompanied by only a vocalist, and at other times by a vocalist and musicians, and at still other times by a drum circle.

A drum circle is a participatory opportunity for the audience to use some of the dozen or so drums provided and follow a leader in a drum pattern.[15] Though not circular, a drum circle implies the initial leader's drum cadence will be copied by all participants. Then slowly another complementary drum pattern will emerge, led by another participant in the drumming assemblage. Soon everyone will follow that pattern, until another pattern harmoniously emerges led by another person. The leaders are not designated, but simply are allowed to emerge. This exercise not only produces a harmonious and beautiful rhythm, but also forces participants to work in accord, carefully considering and copying one another's patterns and then slowly allowing other leadership to emerge. For Christians, the inspirational movements of the Holy Spirit require each participant to listen carefully to how the Holy Spirit is directing other participants, as well as to sense how the Holy Spirit is leading them personally. The overall effect is one of surprising rhythmic beauty, teamwork, spiritual sensitivity, and transference of leadership. There is a well-known saying that if leadership capital is squandered, it is done so at the passing of the baton. Though the author of that adage probably never had a drumming circle in mind, this rhythmic circle affords an auditory and celebratory exercise not only in anointing, but also in the transference of leadership as well.

Inspired Rhythms of Discipleship and the Word

As noted in my first encounter, Solomon's Porch uses improvisation in the proclamation of the Word. This does not mean the sermon is rash or reactive. But after prayer and interaction with other church leaders, Pagitt decides upon a scriptural framework that will provide the bookends to his sermon. The middle is left to develop as the Holy Spirit leads in the evening.

The topics to be addressed also spring forth from the community. A Tuesday night Bible study group may solicit ideas or tender questions. Pagitt usually leads this two- to three-hour discussion each week. But, as with the "musical collaboration," the emergence of the sermon's topic is not limited to this gathering. The sermon comes out of the community's interaction over questions, concerns, and discipleship. The lessons are "drawn from a totally communal approach," reflected church administrator Thomas Karki. "It also happens at the Tuesday men's breakfast. We are constantly in communication with one another, which makes it so refreshing. The sermon is not a product of one man or a Sunday night, but it is a culmination of our conversations all that week."

An Interview with My Tour Guide

Doug Pagitt (*pastor*)

You talk about planning for improvisation. Aren't these mutually exclusive terms?
I don't think so, because improvisation is like jazz. You can only improvise if you first have the right resources, just like a jazz ensemble needs great musicians. This is true of a church and true of jazz. Just winging it means you don't plan. And that's not going to make for good music or good ministry. Rather, improvisation means you have a direction to go and talented people to work with, and you are going to blend those in a particular context.

Improvisation in church is thus not a lack of planning, but an openness to other disciples' input and how the Holy Spirit leads us all. Our improvisations are wonderful mixtures of talents, insights, and synchronization. You have to plan for it, prepare for it, and have a framework first.

So how do you create that framework?
Sunday planning comes out of a communal and collaborative process. At our Tuesday night Bible discussion group, we have a free-flowing discussion about what we are going to cover. The scriptures and their implications are the product of the Holy Spirit working through everyone present that night.

And we talk about implications, rather than applications. We are not trying rigidly to apply a biblical lesson, but we want to understand the implications it has for us. It is like the feeling you get when you answer your phone and there is a state trooper on the other end. This is not a good call. You don't ask how this applies, you ask what are its implications for you. No one asks for a lesson, they ask how this effects or implicates them. What does this mean for me? This is what we are asking. On Tuesdays, we take the implication of a scriptural passage and discuss it, to get our heads around it.

Then on Sunday evenings, we let people respond regarding how the scriptures we have chosen implicate them. We deeply believe in the priesthood of believers. So we rely on the Holy Spirit moving among our community to teach us the implications of this scripture.

This collaborative idea of priesthood extends to all areas of Sunday night. I don't know what songs are picked, what invocation is chosen, how communion is going to be conducted. I rely upon the Holy Spirit to enlighten our leaders. This creates more variety in our evenings, and therefore it can affect more people because we have more voices. Again, it comes out of the deeply held belief in the priesthood of the believer and that everyone who has the Lord in them has something to contribute.

Can such environments lead to heretical ideas?
When I look at church history, it seems to me that heresy comes out of groups with high control. We have a feedback loop. We challenge each other, and speak into our lives. I would be more worried about heresy erupting where disagreement was inhibited. I don't see heresy happening when people listen to another.

To maintain this intimacy, you can't get too big, can you?
You're right. We're discussing that now. We don't think that with the way we do ministry you can become a mega-church. So we're praying about covenant congregations in various areas of town with similar improvised worship issuing forth from an anointed and interdependent leadership.

Any key to improvisation that you wish you'd known coming in?
Yes, I'm still trying to learn how to distinguish between people who have something authentic to share, and those people who just like to listen to themselves. Developing the skill is really hard for someone who feels a responsibility for the evening. For example, there are people who just like to hear themselves talk, and I suppose preachers like myself are the chiefs of sinners here. But I feel really conscious that we don't let things get out of control. I think there has to be a collective

benefit. And thus, you have to develop the skill to ascertain when to stop things and when to let things go. I'm still learning.

Three Lessons to Consider

Lesson 1

Learn the differences between effectiveness and efficiency. The improvisational attitude of Solomon's Porch is really the story of the difference between effectiveness and efficiency. A short primer on the two may be helpful.

Peter Drucker[16] tendered the accepted definition of "effectiveness" as "doing the right things" and "efficiency" as "doing things right."[17] I have come to believe that in this balance the boomer church has focused more on efficiency, that is, doing things right; while the organic church has focused more on effectiveness, that is, "doing the right things." Let me explain.

On the one hand, perhaps in reaction to a *laissez-faire* attitude toward excellence and quality in their parents' (the builders) churches, the boomer church sought to stress "doing things right." Books such as Franky Schaeffer's *Addicted to Mediocrity: 20th Century Christians and the Arts*[18] may have fostered this. Subsequently, boomer churches sought to have the right singers, singing the right songs, with efficient church formats and structures. An overemphasis on professionalism and quality developed. Although this initially may have been a welcome realignment, it has in this researcher's experience led to an overemphasis on efficiency. My consulting work has led me to believe that many boomer churches feel they will be healthy and grow if they just "do things right," usually meaning doing it in a prescribed or franchised manner.

On the other hand, the organic church has sought to regain balance by reintroducing an emphasis on "doing the right things" (effectiveness), rather than just on trying to do things right (efficiency). This distinction becomes especially important when it pertains to worship, which is connecting people to Christ.

Solomon's Porch excels at this connection. The purpose of their experimental approach is to become more effective at connecting people to Christ, rather than following some program or popular strategy that appears to be efficient. My observations led me to believe that the organic church sees effectiveness (connecting people to Christ) as trumping efficiency (doing it in the most programmatic and premeditated way possible). Thus improvisation, with all of its errors, learning curves, bumps, and bruises, must be preferred over a propensity to execute things perfectly. Connection comes out of personal engagement, not out of programmed participation. Drucker agrees, stating, "Effectiveness rather than efficiency is essential . . . the pertinent question is not how to do things right, but how to find the right things to do." In this quest, the organic church is leading the way.

And the organic church recognizes this process will include failures and mistakes. The organic church does not fear such failures, seeing them as lessons regarding what does not work. As such, failure is a learning tool.

The tension between doing the right things (effectiveness) and doing things right (efficiency) leads us to figure 9. On the left, I have listed observed characteristics of churches with incipient institutionalization rising out of an emphasis on doing things right (efficiency). On the right, I have listed observed characteristics of churches using improvisation, fostered by an emphasis on doing the right things (effectiveness).

Figure 9. A Comparison Between
Institutionalization and Improvisation

	Institutionalization	Improvisation
Role of the Holy Spirit	Holy Spirit primarily leads through trained clergy and pastoral office.	Holy Spirit primarily leads through sensitive disciples, both lay and clergy.
	Holy Spirit leads through planned liturgy and field-tested programs.	Holy Spirit can deviate from planned parameters and lead extemporaneously through disciples.
Guidelines and Preparation	Guidelines and preparation dominate and can become dictatorial.	Guidelines and preparation create boundaries and general direction.
Liturgical Elements	Historical litugical elements dominate because they are tried and tested.	Historical elements are usable but can be modified as the moment requires.
Theology	Orthodox theological elements are embraced because of their historical validity.	Orthodox theological elements are embraced because they are effective and work.
Volunteerism	Creates servitude to the model or system. This creates experts.	Creates involvement, creativity, and goal-ownership. This creates artists.
Historical View	Pre-Enlightenment view of the church: churchgoer is ignorant and in need of instruction.	Enlightenment view of the church: churchgoer is an intelligent being made in God's image and in need of guidance.
Missiology	Christians outside the organization (via franchised programs) do the sifting of culture to judge some elements, affirm others, for the transformation of the whole. This creates managers.	Maturing congregants do the sifting of culture to judge some elements, affirm others, for the transformation of the whole. This creates missionaries.

Anointing of the Holy Spirit	Encounter and empowerment of the Holy Spirit increasingly become the experience of planners and not of the congregation.	Encounter and empowermentof the Holy Spirit increasingly become the experience of the congregation.
Self-image (as biblical metaphor[19])	*Temple,* where permanence and stability are esteemed.	*Tabernacle,* an adaptable, movable manifestation of God's glory and presence.
Dangers	(a) Worries over self-preservation can lead to immovability and inflexibility, which create incipient estrangement from one's mission field. (b) Unvarying ritual results in lack of engagement. (c) Venturesome attitude is not required, resulting in less innovation.	(a) Self-interest can foster selfishness and egoism, which may be combated by incipient institutionalization. (b) Unremitting innovation, without selection and evaluation, results in lack of focus. (c) Venturesome attitude is required, but may lessen when under stress or in conflict.
Ethos	Efficiency trumps effectiveness.	Effectiveness trumps efficiency (agree Drucker[20])

Lesson 2

Learn to "improv." Michiko Kakutani's quote that commenced this chapter reminds us that an infatuation with ancient-future elements can lead unknowingly to recycled predictability and triteness. Improvisational originality can thus be a counterbalance. Solomon's Porch embraces improvisation each Sunday, and on the fifth Sunday, attendees improvise beyond their customary parameters. Fifth Sunday experimentation may be a good way to introduce a congregation to this environment of Holy Spirit–infused creativity. To ensure this is done prudently as well as effectively, consider the following three keys to improvisation.

(1) *Prepare.* Preparation may seem contradictory to improvisation, but actually it is the most important element. Improvisation in worship must have a goal. And it should start with a biblical one, to "love the Lord your God with all your heart and with all your soul and with all your mind" (Matthew 22:37), doing so "in spirit and truth" (John 4:23). Thus, improvisation begins with this objective, to connect people with God in essential and authentic ways. Collaboration follows, requiring prayer, advice from mature disciples, and an understanding of God's vision for the future of a congregation. Then, the general parameters of the experience can be mapped out, including customary features. At Solomon's Porch, several recurring features provide a general framework: scripture and potential implications, worship that is fresh and germane, prayer, and communion.

(2) *Present and guide.* The presentation must be conducted without tyranny. Solomon's Porch uses a consensus among mature leaders to guide its improvisational environment. But as Pagitt noted, distinguishing between when someone has something to say from God, or something that originates from self, can be a challenge. Improvisation, however, creates a powerful communal experience, which Viola Spolin describes as "the sharing (union), give and take, of each and every one's excitement, experience and intuitive energy."[21]

(3) *Debrief.* Improvisation is not only potent, but also as noted above, potentially abused. Allow mature Christians to evaluate and discuss the outcome. Remember, improvisation is not just winging it; but a premeditated foray into God's Word and its implications for his children. As Spolin explains, "Evaluation . . . is the time to establish an objective vocabulary, and direct communication made possible through non-judgmental attitudes, group assistance in solving a problem, and clarification of the focus of an exercise."[22]

Lesson 3

Release your innovation gene. As a human gene can reside veiled and obscure in an organism, innovation is a talent that can lie underdeveloped in a Christian community until released. To release this innovation in a timely as well as diplomatic manner, the following three steps have been adapted from Hamel and Skarzynski's work on ingenuity.[23]

(1) *Innovation doesn't follow a schedule.* Though Solomon's Porch uses a Wednesday evening "musical collaboration" to craft fresh songs for the upcoming Sunday, church administrator Thomas Karki was quick to point out, "But that's just one venue. Creativity happens throughout our community. Songs may come out of a Bible discussion group, from a ministry event, from personal reflection, anywhere. Songs come out of our community, from out of a place." Don't think you can schedule a time or place for creativity to rise. Rather, see the entire rhythm of the community to be one where creativity can arise from the least likely places. Nokia launched its successful line of rainbow colored mobile phones, not after a daylong strategy meeting, but after an afternoon when company execs lunched near California's Venice Beach and noticed sun-drenched skaters awash in colorful clothes.[24]

(2) *Shatter the innovation monopoly.* Innovation and creativity arise from fresh, imaginative, and diverse environs. Thus, Hamel and Skarzynski discovered that innovation wanes if controlled by a small leadership segment. Many seeker-church models may unintentionally do this when they designate "creative teams" to design artistic environments for worship gatherings. My experience has led me to agree, for I have noticed the longer creative teams exist, the less innovation results. Thus, it is important to encourage creativity to come from all segments of a congregation. Unlock and then welcome ideas from across the community. Legendary British entrepreneur Richard Branson encourages employees of his Virgin Enterprises to email him with ideas. Thus, when a Virgin Airlines flight attendant had trouble planning her own wedding, she pitched the idea of a wedding planning

boutique to Branson, which eventually resulted in a successful new enterprise.

(3) *Build a safe place for people to innovate.* Darrell Guder pointed out that much like the temple in the Old Testament, today's Christian community often becomes an immovable, inflexible, and ostentatious environment. Consequently, the church inadvertently distances itself from the people it is trying to serve. Instead, Guder believes a better biblical metaphor for a church is that of the tabernacle, an adaptable, movable manifestation of God's glory and presence.[25] The flexibility and movability of a tabernacle best describes how the outward manifestation (that is, the methodology) of the good news may innovatively adapt, but the central essence, doctrine, and principles of the tabernacle's purpose do not change with its adaptable encasement.

Thus, Christian communities must become safe, even welcoming places for innovation to be tendered and shared. Solomon's Porch does this by welcoming ideas from all community quarters, even from the floor during sermons. While some churches may shy away from this due to the potential for dissenting thoughts arising from the floor, Solomon's Porch sees this as an opportunity to engage in discussion with modern philosophies and apply God's truth. And they do so in much the same way that the early church engaged Hellenistic philosophical ideas—at Solomon's Porch.

CHAPTER 13

Nurturing an Organic Congregation: The Leadership Collage

This (organic) metaphor should remind you that different types of organizational species will face different demands and respond in different ways. Thus, there can be no best way of organizing that will work equally well for all organizations.
—Mary Jo Hatch, organization theorist [1]

The Organic Uniqueness

Organic, by its very, nature cannot be manufactured, but must be grown, nurtured, and cultivated from the fabric of life. This travelogue has been an exploratory look at such natural components cultivated in twelve organic congregations.

However, to foster an organic organization requires the perception, patience, and sheer dogged persistence of a farmer. Perhaps this is why Jesus' metaphors often appeared in agricultural contexts, for the farmer possibly more so than the merchant, soldier, or priest understood the organic nature of growth within God's kingdom.

Thus, to nurture an organic organization requires avoiding the temptation to apply mechanically the three lessons described in each chapter. Rather, the authentic leader approaches the task in phases, much like seasons. To symbolize visually this organic development, I have created figure 10.

Figure 10. The Four Seasons of Organic Leadership

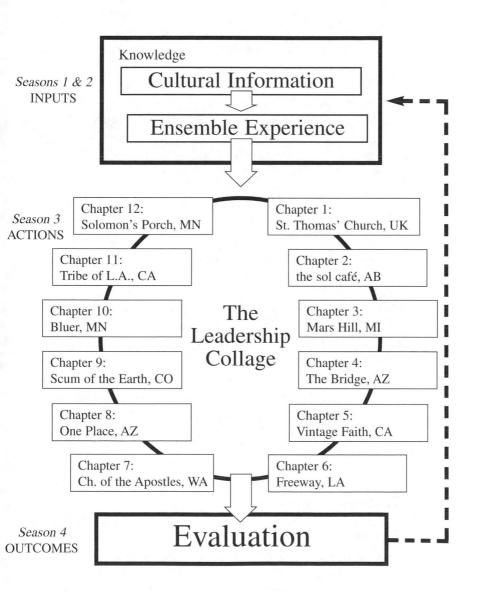

Seasons 1 & 2
INPUTS

Knowledge

Cultural Information

Ensemble Experience

Season 3
ACTIONS

Chapter 12:
Solomon's Porch, MN

Chapter 1:
St. Thomas' Church, UK

Chapter 11:
Tribe of L.A., CA

Chapter 2:
the sol café, AB

Chapter 10:
Bluer, MN

The
Leadership
Collage

Chapter 3:
Mars Hill, MI

Chapter 9:
Scum of the Earth, CO

Chapter 4:
The Bridge, AZ

Chapter 8:
One Place, AZ

Chapter 5:
Vintage Faith, CA

Chapter 7:
Ch. of the Apostles, WA

Chapter 6:
Freeway, LA

Season 4
OUTCOMES

Evaluation

Season 1: Cultural Information

As I interviewed leaders of organic churches, I found that most had studied the philosophies and structures behind postmodernism, as well as postmodernal church expressions, before launching their endeavors. Thus, the church leader wishing effectively to engage an unchurched and postmodern culture should first spend a season in reflection, contemplation, and study. Books on these topics are published with great regularity. As such, to cite the best in this current volume would be fruitless. However, the following are suggested avenues for building your cultural knowledge base.

Building a Knowledge Base for an Organic Endeavor

(1) Begin by perusing bibliographies of college and seminary courses that deal with postmodernism (many are available online). Professors are customarily acquainted with contemporary perspectives, and their bibliographies usually cite up-to-date writings.

(2) Find out what young people are watching, reading, and discussing. Spend time with a focus group of young adults dissecting their philosophies of life, the books they are reading, the media they are watching, the magazines they peruse, and the ethical, theological, and philosophical debates they pursue.

(3) Search online blogs. Blogs are ongoing Web diaries about every topic imaginable. Online blogs dealing with postmodern thought are especially helpful. To search these discussions, visit a Web site that hosts such blogs and search using keywords.

(4) Develop reading lists of popular and/or influential secular and Christian books on postmodern thinking. Publishers' catalogues and bookstores (both online and onsite) are helpful.

(5) Engage postmodern thinkers. Begin a person-to-person, online, or written dialogue with persons engaged in postmodern thought. Postmodern researcher Mary Jo Hatch found that oftentimes such thinkers are artists who reflect their philosophies in their art and its interpretation.[2] Use the following two guidelines to engage these thinkers diplomatically.

(a) Do not try to change their mind. At this stage, your cultural understanding is usually too underdeveloped to engage effectively a postmodern thinker. You are still at the informational stage, gathering pertinent knowledge.

(b) Do not judge or sermonize. Again, a rudimentary understanding means that you are not sufficiently informed to engage in sophisticated dialogue or persuasive argument.

Season 2: The Ensemble Experience

Head and Heart Knowledge

Seasons 1 and 2 comprise the "inputs," or "sources," for knowledge of the organic worldview. But, while *cultural information* contributes to "head knowledge," the *ensemble experience* adds to "heart knowledge." Regrettably, head knowledge alone often leads to unsympathetic and inaccurate assessments. The ensemble experience thus differs from the cultural information stage because the *joie de vivre*—community and aesthetics of a postmodern environment—is experienced firsthand.

To assist in such experiences, the "dashboards" that commence chapters 1-12 give contact information for each organization. But as mentioned in the "Prelude," the evolutionary nature of these congregations means they will have changed since this author's visit. Thus, use this book as a roadside snapshot, reflecting a moment in time, and a starting place to map out your own journey.

Charting Your Trip

The following resources can be helpful in mapping out your journey.

(1) Organic churches communicate through electronic media, and thus the Internet contains numerous listings of organic congregations. Three of the best sites are www.theooze.com, www.emergingchurch.org, and www.theorganicchurch.org.

(2) Look in regional newspapers and entertainment tabloids aimed at young people for advertisements of organic

churches geared to the postmodern mind-set. You won't find organic church advertisements on the church page. However, you often will find them amid advertisements for bars, rock concerts, and restaurants. Organic church leaders tend to feel that their community should be an integrated part of life and not segregated to a church sector. While sitting in the Memphis airport, I picked up an airport version of an entertainment tabloid and quickly found two organic congregations thriving in the area.

(3) Check with denominational and judicatory sources. Many mainline denominations have flourishing organic congregations.

(4) Contact organic communities and inquire about congregations in your area.

(5) Post your questions regarding locations on appropriate Web logs, or blogs. Organic church blogs offer an ever-widening group of discussants with extensive connections.

Lingering and Reoccurring Melodies of the Organic Church

Reoccurring themes will emerge during your journey. Such commonalities are described in the section entitled "The Finale" that began this book. However, the following is a brief overview.

Four Melodies Behind the Organic Church

(1) *The Melody of Orthodoxy.* Some cultural observers have wondered if organic churches reject the Bible's grand narrative of redemption in Jesus Christ. In my encounters, I found this not to be the case. Each congregation reflected the basic suppositions of orthodox theology held by its sponsoring or affiliated organization.

(2) *The Melody of Authenticity.* The organic church offers an important course correction to a boomer church that often strays too far toward professionalism and mechanicalism. This boomer propensity is replaced by the organic church's ability to create unique rhythmic and evolutionary fusions of leadership principles, skills, and experiences. This is also reflected in their worship

and ministry, which is based on a genuine sense of God's presence and participation. And since such spirituality is authentic and not contrived, they do not hesitate to let peers observe their experiential praise, reintroducing what some commentators have called "unashamed spirituality." [3]

(3) *The Melody of Engagement: Social and Spiritual.* The organic church believes in concurrently meeting the social needs and spiritual needs of a community. They are not content to follow boomer tactics, in which individual churches typically excel at one or the other. Organic churches see Christ's mandate to meet the physical needs of creation as cocqual and conecessary with his mandate to meet humankind's need for salvation. They will not, in the name of tactics, separate the cultural and evangelistic mandates.

(4) *The Melody of Missional Church Growth.* Organic churches understand the advantages and abuse inherent in church growth thinking. Subsequently, they focus on the healthy aspects of church growth by stressing its missionary approach toward engaging modern societies. The approach is sometimes called the "missional church" perspective, for it returns classical church growth thinking to its missionary roots, recapturing a missionary orientation towards today's mosaic of cultures.

Making Tomorrow's Music Today; Three Melodies for the Future

The following are introduced here for the first time, for they are future melodies that the reader will notice rising from this book's illustrations.

(1) *The Melody of Persistence.* The organic church is here to stay. Every time I visit a city in which one organic church has died, I find two to four more have sprung up to replace it. The hunger of young people to indigenize church for their own styles and sensibilities will not subside with time anymore than a boomer propensity to embrace contemporary music has waned over the years.

(2) *A Variety of Melodies:*

(a) *They Come in Many Sizes.* Though by their very nature the interpersonal character and connectedness of the organic church keeps many small in size, other organic churches have grown to mega-church proportions (e.g. Mars Hill and St. Thomas/The Philadelphia Churches). They do so by maintaining intimacy while expanding (usually through extensive small group networks).

(b) *They Come with Many Affiliations and Styles.* The high-church liturgy of its Episcopal affiliation fosters liturgical elements, albeit updated and musically progressive, at Church of the Apostles in Seattle. And the Southern Baptist roots of The Bridge in Phoenix color its message and altar/prayer ministry. This diversity resonates from this book's many illustrations.

(3) *The Melody of Replication.* The organic church provides a wonderful example of holistic communities allied in faith, service, and mission. Their examples have infused worship and ministry with new, relevant elements or reinterpretations of traditions that for many have recaptured relevant and engaging ministry. The church universal, which in many cases has moved away from its authentic roots due to time, tedium, or busyness, can infuse in its congregations some of this initial euphoria by indigenizing the lessons from the organic church. This may take many forms, but some examples might include:

(a) Adding an organic worshiping community to a church's more traditional and contemporary worship expressions/communities.

(b) Creating opportunities, such as a gallery in the church, where all artists, including those whose preferred media are oils, photography, sculpture, and mixed-media, can honor God with their skills.

(c) Creating a more closely balanced ministry to meet people's physical needs (the cultural mandate), while also meeting their need for salvation (the evangelistic mandate).

(d) Including more diverse and global forms, symbols, and stories in worship and ministry.

(e) Nurturing an organic offspring community, either as a subcongregation[4] or a daughter community.[5]

Season 3: The Leadership Collage

Organic Is a Significant Metaphor

After experiencing the life, interdependence, and vitality of organic communities, the sojourner becomes aware that the organic metaphor is apropos for the following reasons:

(1) The word *organic* describes an organization that "is dependent upon its environment for the resources that support life."[6]

(2) In organic systems, all parts work together.

(3) Organic organisms adapt to their environment.

(4) And, because organically different species live in different environments and respond differently, "thus there can be no one best way of organizing that will work equally well for all organizations."[7]

Your Leadership Collage: Multiple Parts and Multiple Perspectives

To lead an organic organization requires an elastic mixture of leadership skills and perspectives. Mary Jo Hatch discovered that effective postmodern leaders create a collage from the tools and practices that best suit their situations and skills. She defines a collage as:

> an art form in which objects and pieces of objects (often including reproductions of other works of art . . .) are arranged together to form something new—an art object in its own right. When you use collage as a metaphor for organization theory you are recognizing the value of holding multiple perspectives and using parts of theories to form a new work . . . they (postmodern leaders) use

bits of old theories along with the knowledge and experience they have collected in their lifetimes to create a new theory worthy of use in particular circumstances.[8]

Hatch found that effective postmodern leaders pick and choose from a patchwork (some might say hodgepodge) of individually valuable components that the leader combines to create a new and appealing expression.

Creating Your Leadership Collage

To fashion a leadership collage:

(1) Create a collage as a team. Teamwork produces corrections in course, creative new synergies, and goal ownership.

(2) Assess the circumstances that surround your church (sometimes called *external environments*), as well as your organization's internal situations (sometimes called *internal environments*).

(a) External environments are the sociocultural, economic, political, technological, political/legal, and demographic forces that are outside of the control of your organization and to which an organization must react.[9]

(b) Internal environments are programs, ministries, strategies, strengths, weaknesses, or any other factors over which the church has direct control. They can include finances, assets, resources, disunity, unity, volunteer power, staffing levels, programs, and so on.

(3) Next, investigate which principles, ideas, and perspectives are best suited to your external and internal environments.

(a) You may wish to begin by looking at the case studies in this book. Each chapter includes three lessons or principles that might be adaptable to your environments. Ask yourself which ideas from each chapter build best upon your external and internal situations. The *circle,* titled "The Four Seasons of Organic Leadership" in figure 10, represents the elements from which a collage may be created.

(b) Look to your own personal experience. What has experience and God's guidance prepared you to use or reconstitute?

(4) Experiment with as many parts and perspectives as appropriate. Be careful here. This is not permission to experiment uncritically. Rather, draw upon your leadership team and the multiple perspectives available to craft an experimental process, that is, one that is open to revision.

(5) Move forward purposely, yet not hastily. In an earlier book titled *Staying Power,* I explained how churches polarize over change, usually because those pushing for change do so too rapidly and do so before getting reticent power brokers on board. Consult *Staying Power* to navigate the six stages and five triggers of change that keep change from becoming divisive.[10]

Finally, the concept of a leadership collage fits nicely with the organic metaphor. Hatch points out that "this (organic) metaphor should remind you that different types of organizational species will face different demands and respond in different ways."[11] Thus, the leadership collage paints a mental picture of an indigenous, elastic, and organic approach.

Season 4: Evaluation

Postmodern young people typically think of knowledge as "inherently unstable,"[12] a perception that has probably risen due to startling advances in science and technology. As a result, postmodernists embrace natural adaptation through ongoing evaluation as a way to stay relevant.

I have discovered that in the organic church evaluation is carried out with the same vigor that their boomer parents embraced step-by-step planning. Postmodernists often believe lockstep planning is ineffective, too regimented, and inflexible; yet conversely feel that ongoing evaluation results in upgrading and enhancement. Management guru Peter Drucker warned that "unless strategy evaluation is performed seriously and systematically, and unless strategists are willing to act on the results, energy will be used up defending yesterday."[13] Organic church leaders seem intuitively to understand this temptation to avoid evaluation and canonize yesterday's practices.

Evaluation can take place through interviews of those involved, as well as with those to whom ministry is directed. Focus groups can provide helpful feedback and correction in course. However, evaluation is wasted if it does not lead to rethinking what I have labeled in Figure 10 as Seasons 1 and 2: Knowledge.

Organic Conclusions

An organism is unique, growing out of a one-of-a-kind symbiosis of its parts. In addition, an organism adapts to its environment, further making it an elastic and synergetic partnership. Thus, organic leadership teams must—through knowledge, experience, strategy, and evaluation—uncover the leadership collages that will empower and proliferate their organic community.

CHAPTER 14

Final Postcards from the Road

To my organic sojourners:

Thank you for including me in your journeys and communities. And though you have graciously embraced much of my analysis, at those times when you disagreed you always afforded respect.

Your efforts to return to authenticity and originality in areas of spiritual growth, worship, and discipleship have reminded me of the milieu in which I became Christian, some thirty years ago. I hope that you will avoid the digressions into which I and my boomer colleagues succumbed. Our initial elation and innovation mirrored yours, but over time it became codified and entrenched.

Yet, your sincere and authentic experiments have reminded me of what my church experience once was, and which I long to know again.

To my boomer colleagues:

I sense the organic church has recaptured the renewal many of us experienced in the 1970s and 1980s. And though time and languor has emaciated this regeneration, it may be through engaging the organic church that we can recapture an authentic and innovative expression of an unchanging gospel. Moreover, I ask that you remember and replicate the actions of those who altruistically helped us in the early days of our experiment.

To my students and colleagues at Indiana Wesleyan University:

I thank you for you flexibility, probing thoughts, participation, and prayers. Our Master of Arts in Ministry students have been especially valuable. And thus, my gracious thanks goes to my school for being a sponsor of this journey.

And finally, to my Lord Jesus and my family:

Thank you for making this trek possible and for helping me see ever more clearly the harvest through God's eyes.

Because of all of you, I'm back on the road again . . . carried by God's wind. "The wind blows wherever it pleases. You hear its sound, but you cannot tell where it comes from or where it is going. So it is with everyone born of the Spirit" (John 3:8).

NOTES

The Finale: Conclusions

1. Though the degree of ecclesial imprudence found in the boomer church does not approximate the depth of Babylonian degradation, the parallel need for reappraisal, reconnection, and authentic revitalization is valid.

2. I define "orthodoxy" as religious belief that confirms and conforms to the Niceno-Constantinopolitan Creed as formulated at the First Ecumenical Council at Nicea in AD 325, and as expanded in the Second Ecumenical Council at Constantinople in AD 381.

3. A common viewpoint within postmodern philosophy is that all so-called meta-narratives are insufficient and thus should be rejected. A leading proponent of this, Jean-Francois Lyotard, argued that the "modern age" sought large-scale explanations, or meta-narratives, that could explain the nature of the universe, epistemology, economics, and religion (*The Postmodern Condition: A Report of Knowledge,* trans. Geoff Bennington and Brian Massumi, in *Theory and History of Literature,* vol. 1 [Minneapolis: University of Minnesota Press, 1984], xxiii, 6). However, Lyotard argued the subsequent postmodern age found these meta-explanations insufficiently flexible, indigenous, and valid; and subsequently the critical mind must relegate meta-narratives to the outmoded age of modernity (Ibid., xxiii). For Lyotard, these outmoded meta-narratives include scientific narratives (for example, the unified field theory), economic narratives (for example, economic determinism), as well as religious meta-narratives (for example, the biblical good news). While a rejection of meta-narratives is widely embraced by postmodern philosophers, I did not find in the emerging organic church a rejection of the good news meta-narrative pervasive or even evident. An apprehension that this will or may be the case has not surfaced in my travels among the organic church.

137

4. Donald A. McGavran was the missiologist and former dean of the School of World Mission at Fuller Seminary who suggested that we scrutinize the effectiveness of the evangelical mission in North America with the same veracity that we analyze foreign mission endeavors. It was largely through McGavran's work and that of his pupils that the Church Growth Movement was birthed. It surprised this author to find in these emerging congregations a widespread understanding and appreciation for classic church growth strategies as elucidated by McGavran and his successors.

5. Sociologist George Ritzer described this boomer proclivity for franchising generic programming as the "McDonaldization of Western culture" (*The McDonaldization of Society: An Investigation into the Changing Character of Contemporary Social Life*, rev. ed. [Thousand Oaks, Calif.: Pine Forge Press, 1996]). Scottish clergyman John Drane builds upon Ritzer's critiques, indigenizing them for the church in his cautionary tome, *The McDonaldization of the Church: Consumer Culture and the Church's Future* (Macon, Ga.: Smyth & Helwys Publishing, 2001).

6. Arthur F. Glasser, "Confession, Church Growth, and Authentic Unity in Missionary Strategy," *Protestant Crosscurrents in Mission*, ed. Norman A. Horner (Nashville: Abingdon Press, 1968), 178-221.

7. C. Peter Wagner, *Church Growth and the Whole Gospel: A Biblical Mandate* (New York: Harper & Row, 1981), 13.

8. Ibid., 14.

9. C. Peter Wagner, in *On the Crest of the Wave: Becoming a World Christian* (Ventura, Calif.: Regal Books, 1983), crafts a helpful diagram (pp. 45-47) describing how different churches try to prioritize and balance, often ineffectively, the cultural and the evangelistic mandate.

10. The duality of the church's mission has always been at the heart of the Great Commission. In his book on church growth strategy, Pete Wagner argued that the evangelistic mandate (to bring all persons to a saving knowledge of Christ) is incomplete without bestowing the social mandate (to meet the physical and emotional needs of those we seek to reach): "True Christian compassion does not erect false dichotomies which separate body and soul. . . . If I love my neighbor, I will want to see him fed, clothed, cured and well adjusted. I will want to see also that he is not going to hell, doomed to an eternity separated from God" (*Frontiers in Missionary Strategy* [Chicago: Moody Press, 1971], 37). This integrated nature of the evangelical mandate (as exemplified in the Great Commission in Matthew 28:19-20) and the cultural mandate (as stated in the Great Commandment in Matthew 22:37-39) has been theoretically accepted by boomer churches, but, sadly, inconsistently or insufficiently practiced by most.

11. Donald A. McGavran, *Understanding Church Growth* (Grand Rapids: William B. Eerdmans Publishing Company, 1970), 25.

12. Darrell L. Guder, ed., *Missional Church: A Vision for the Sending of the Church in North America* (Grand Rapids: William B. Eerdmans Publishing Company, 1998).

13. Ibid., 2.

14. Lesslie Newbigin, *The Other Side of 1984: Questions for the Churches* (New York: National Council of Churches, 1984).

15. Guder, *Missional Church*, 4-5.

The Prelude: An Overview of My Travels

1. Sociologists often divide generations into convenient nineteen-year seg-ments for analysis and description. To aid in retention, these generations are often given short illustrative appellations by the media. As such, the baby boom generation was so named because it signified an upswing in births following the Second World War. Sometimes shortened to just "boomers," the name was bor-rowed from Old West parlance in which a boomtown was a settlement that exploded overnight due to the discovery of gold or silver. The boomers exploded onto the scene in 1946 and continued to 1964. The generation born between 1965 and 1983 was labeled Generation X, a term that may have its genesis in a boomer critique of this generation as somewhat nihilistic and casual. During my journey a relaxed attitude was evident, but nihilism was not. In fact, I have found Generation X not to be the disengaged generation the boomers predicted, but rather a genuinely honest and appealing generation with a passion for righting boomer ills and recapturing authentic worship encounters. It is this dual passion that drives much of these emerging organic church experiments. The parents of the boomers have been called the "greatest generation" by Tom Brokaw in his best-selling book by the same name (New York: Random House, 1998). Still, many generational writers and researchers call it the "Builder Generation" (Gary McIntosh, *One Church Four Generations: Understanding and Reaching All Ages in Your Church* [Grand Rapids: Baker, 2002]; Bob Whitesel and Kent R. Hunter in *A House Divided: Bridging the Generation Gaps in Your Church* [Nashville: Abingdon Press, 2000]). In this book, I will follow the builder termi-nology, for it connotes that it built the United States into a worldwide military and economic power. And finally, the generation that will replace Generation X is often called Generation Y; partly because a suitable descriptor has not yet been found, and additionally to denote a succession with Generation X. Thus, for this present volume, Generation Y will be used. Below is a chart that depicts the interrelationships of these generations by year of birth:

Figure 11. Generations and Their Birth Years

Birth Years:	Age in 2006:	Sociological Designation:
1945 and before	61+	Builders
1946–1964	42–60	(Baby) Boomers
1965–1983	23–41	Generation X
	(32–41)	(Leading Edge Gen. X)
	(23–31)	(Emergent Gen. X)
1984–2002	4–22	Generation Y

2. Eddie Gibbs points out in *ChurchNext: Quantum Changes in How We Do Ministry* (Downers Grove, Ill.: InterVarsity Press, 2000) that it was Frederico de Onis who coined the term "postmodern" in the 1930s (p. 23). However, it did not garner widespread acceptance until used in the 1960s by art critics.

3. Quoted in *Questions That Matter: An Invitation to Philosophy,* 4th ed., by Ed L. Miller (New York: McGraw-Hill, 1996), 199.

4. Abridged by Alvin Plantinga, "The Twin Pillars of Christian Scholarship," in *The Stob Lectures of Calvin College and Seminary, 1989–1990.* Rorty is also famous for stating that "great edifying philosophers destroy for the sake of their own generation," meaning that philosophy must be reinterpreted by each generation (*Philosophy and the Mirror of Nature* [Princeton, N.J.: Princeton University Press, 1979], 369). This viewpoint led to the term "deconstructionist," which further alarms boomers that emerging congregations will attempt to deconstruct truth. However, in my travels among the organic church, I have not found their deconstructionism to be aimed at theology, but only at cultural preferences and modes.

5. John Leland, "Hip New Churches Pray to a Different Drummer," *The New York Times,* February 18, 2004. Leland states, "The congregations vary in denomination, but most are from the evangelical side of Protestantism."

6. Eddie Gibbs and Ryan Bolger, "Tracking the Emerging Church," *Journal of the American Society for Church Growth* (Winter 2004): 4.

7. Charles B. Singletary, "Organic Growth: A Critical Dimension for the Church," in *Church Growth State of the Art,* ed. C. Peter Wagner, with Win Arn and Elmer Towns (Wheaton, Ill.: Tyndale House Publishers, 1986), 114.

8. Alan Roxburgh, "Missional Leadership: Equipping God's People for Mission," in *Missional Church: A Vision for the Sending of the Church in North America,* ed. Darrell L. Guder (Grand Rapids: William B. Eerdmans Publishing Company, 1998), 193.

9. Howard Snyder, *The Problem of Wine Skins* (Downers Grove, Ill.: InterVarsity Press, 1975), 157.

10. James F. Engel, *Contemporary Christian Communication: Its Theory and Practice* (Nashville: Thomas Nelson, 1979), 93-95.

11. Alistair Davidson, *Antonio Gramsci: Towards an Intellectual Biography* (Atlantic Highlands, N.J.: Humanities Press, 1977). Though a Marxist theorist, Antonio Gramsci argued that the revolutionary model developed by Lenin would not survive in Europe. Regardless of Gramsci's revolutionary bent, his understanding of the role of "organic" intellectuals in explaining grand ideas to modern cultures has secured his status within the social sciences.

12. David O. Moberg, in *The Church as Social Institution: The Sociology of American Religion* ([Englewood Cliffs, N.J.: Prentice Hall, 1962], 119-23), outlines his theory of institutional life cycles, shedding light on how renewal networks often migrate from functional to marginal.

13. "Nonorganic" will be used to distinguish churches that do not possess a significant number of the patterns of the organic church. Typically, these nonorganic churches will be programmatic in orientation, focused more on outcomes than on encounter or the journey. Though often these nonorganic congregations will be boomer congregations, some will be those that through affiliation, cultural interaction, or encounter are slowly adopting many of the characteristics of the organic church.

14. H. Richard Niebuhr, *Christ and Culture* (New York: Harper & Brothers, 1951).

15. Charles H. Kraft, *Christianity in Culture: A Study in Dynamic Biblical Theologizing in Cross-Cultural Perspective* (Maryknoll, N.Y.: Orbis Books, 2005).

16. Lesslie Newbigin, *The Gospel in a Pluralist Society* (Grand Rapids: Eerdmans, 1989).

17. Craig Van Gelder, "Understanding North American Culture," in *Missional Church: A Vision for the Sending of the Church in North America*, ed. Darrell L. Guder (Grand Rapids: William B. Eerdmans Publishing Company, 1990), 37.

18. Gibbs, *ChurchNext*, 25.

19. These reactions were culled from my sojourns among the organic church and will be expounded and expanded in the following chapters of this travelogue.

20. For more on how to evaluate and end ineffective programming, see chap. 7, "Missteps with Evaluation," in my book *Growth by Accident, Death by Planning: How Not to Kill a Growing Congregation* (Nashville: Abingdon Press, 2004), 97-107.

21. Robert Banks, "Time: The New Commodity," in *Strategies for Today's Leader*, vol. XXXIII, no. 1 (1996): 13.

1. St. Thomas' Church, Sheffield, England

1. Søren Kierkegaard, *The Sickness unto Death: A Christian Psychological Exposition for Upbuilding and Awakening* (Princeton, N.J.: Princeton University Press, 1980), 103.

2. English researcher Peter Brierley has compared British census data against church attendance to calculate that an average of 2,200 people leave the Church of England each week (*The Tide Is Running Out* [London: Christian Research, 2000], 129).

3. See Darrell Guder, et. al, *Missional Church: A Vision for the Sending of the Church in North America* (Grand Rapids: William B. Eerdmans Publishing Company, 1998); and Eddie Gibbs, *ChurchNext: Quantum Changes in How We Do Ministry,* (Downers Grove, Ill.: InterVarsity Press, 2000).

4. St. Thomas' Church of Crookes, *The Order of Mission: An Introductory Guide* (Sheffield, England, n.d.).

5. Paddy Mallon, *Calling a City Back to God* (Eastbourne: Kingsway Communications, 2003), 38.

6. The genesis of today's icon-driven culture may have emerged in the scientific model and its accompanying scientific notation.

7. Mallon, *Calling a City*, 140, notes that Breen based the four phases of leadership development upon ideas gleaned from Kenneth Blanchard's *The One Minute Manager* (New York: Harper Collins, 1985), 46-58.

8. Mallon, *Calling a City*, 36.

9. Chosen to replace Mike Breen at Saint Thomas' Church, Mick Woodhead had previously been the vicar of a nearby growing Anglican congregation and prior to his call to ministry was an engineer for eighteen years.

10. Mike Breen's passion for serving young generations has resulted in the release of two books on the Lifeshapes© principles, *A Passionate Life* (Colorado Springs, Colo: Cook Publishing, 2005), and *The Passionate Church* (Colorado Springs, Colo: Cook Publishing, 2004). Information is also available at www.lifeshapes.com.

11. Clark H. Pinnock, *Set Forth Your Case: An Examination of Christianity's Credentials* (Chicago: Moody Press, 1971).

12. George G. Hunter, *The Contagious Congregation: Frontiers in Evangelism and Church Growth* (Nashville: Abingdon Press, 1979), 63.

13. To unite your subcongregations, design unity events, and retain a small-church feel while you reach out, consult Bob Whitesel and Kent R. Hunter, *A House Divided: Bridging the Generation Gaps in Your Church* (Nashville: Abingdon Press, 2000); and Bob Whitesel, *Staying Power: Why People Leave the Church Over Change and What You Can Do About It* (Nashville: Abingdon Press, 2003).

2. the sol café, Edmonton, Alberta, Canada

1. Sally Morgenthaler, "Film and Worship: Windows in Caves and Other Things We Do with Perfectly Good Prisms," *Theology, News and Notes,* vol. 52, no. 2 (2005), 25.

2. The sol café's leaders appropriated their name from the book *A Cup of Coffee at the Soul Café* by Leonard I. Sweet and Denise Marie Siino (Nashville: Broadman & Holman Publishers, 1998). They also modified it to fit the bilingual culture of Canada.

3. The incorporated name of the church is "the sol café," with each word in lowercase.

4. Christian and Missionary Alliance of Canada, the denominational affiliation of the sol café congregation.

5. Eddie Gibbs, *ChurchNext: Quantum Changes in How We Do Ministry* (Downers Grove, Ill.: InterVarsity Press, 2000), 235.

6. Ihab Habib Hassan has tendered a well-known list of postmodern reactions to modernity. In that list, he sees "chance" as a postmodern reaction to modernity's "design," and "participation" as a reaction to "distance." The interactive dialogue during organic church sermons seems to support Hassan's conclusions regarding these distinctives. *The Dismemberment of Orpheus: Toward a Postmodern Literature,* 2nd ed. (Madison: University of Wisconsin Press, 1982), 267.

7. Alan Roxburgh, "Equipping God's People for Mission" in *Missional Church: A Vision for the Sending of the Church in North America,* ed. Darrell Guder (Grand Rapids: William B. Eerdmans Publishing Company, 1998), 198.

3. Mars Hill, Grandville, Michigan

1. Stjepan G. Mestrovic, *Postemotional Society* (London: SAGE Publications, 1997), 95. This is Mestrovic's summation of Ferdinand Tönnies's classic arguments on the distinctions between communities and societies in *Community and Society* (New York: Harper & Row, [1887] 1963).

2. Former city planner turned church growth consultant Lyle Schaller tendered the first well-known classifications of church size. He labeled churches of over seven hundred attendees as "mini-denominations," since they function as a network of subcongregations (Lyle E. Schaller, *The Multiple Staff and the Larger Church* [Nashville: Abingdon Press, 1980], 28; see also George G.

Hunter III, *The Contagious Congregation: Frontiers in Evangelism and Church Growth* [Nashville: Abingdon Press, 1979], 63). Gary McIntosh, in his book *One Size Doesn't Fit All: Bringing Out the Best in Any Size Church* ([Grand Rapids, Mich.: Fleming H. Revell, 1999], 17-19), labels churches of more than four hundred attendees "large" and notes the "organizational basis" of their focus. Although these labels are better descriptors for ecclesial management, the more trendy mega-church label has prevailed in popular culture and customarily describes a church of more than one thousand weekend attendees.

3. Messages at Mars Hill deal unswervingly with the challenges of living in a postmodern world. A recent sermon title was "The Revolutionary Life in an Abercrombie and Fitch World: Exploring Sexuality, Lust, and the Culture of Skin We Live In" (www.mhbcmi.org, 2004).

4. The theatre-in-the-round environment is employed not only at Mars Hill, but also at Solomon's Porch in Minneapolis.

5. ©2004, 2005 Mars Hill, and adapted from their website: www.mhbcmi.org/about/directions.php

6. Ibid.

7. H. Richard Niebuhr, *Christ and Culture* (New York: Harper & Brothers, 1951), 195.

8. www.mhbcmi.org/about/directions.php

9. Ibid.

10. Ibid.

11. Niebuhr, *Christ and Culture,* 194.

12. Donald A. McGavran with Win C. Arn, *How to Grow a Church: Conversations About Church Growth* (Glendale, Calif.: G/L Publications, 1973), 115.

13. Lyle E. Schaller, *Effective Church Planning* (Nashville: Abingdon Press, 1981), 17-63; C. Peter Wagner, *Your Church Can Grow,* rev. ed. (Ventura, Calif.: Regal Books, 1984), 107-8; Eddie Gibbs, *I Believe in Church Growth* (Grand Rapids, Mich.: William B. Eerdmans Publishing Company, 1981), 275-82.

14. Bob Whitesel and Kent R. Hunter, *A House Divided: Bridging the Generation Gaps in Your Church* (Nashville: Abingdon Press, 2000), 26.

15. Bob Whitesel, *Growth by Accident, Death by Planning: How Not to Kill a Growing Congregation* (Nashville: Abingdon Press, 2004), 140.

16. Small groups can be, but are not limited to: Sunday school classes, leadership committees, training classes, classes of any kind, prayer groups, praise teams, and any kind of church team (ministry, fellowship, or athletic oriented). For more information, see "Missteps with Small Groups," chap. 1 in my book *Growth by Accident,* 133-51.

17. Peter W. Brierley, *The Tide Is Running Out: What the English Church Attendance Survey Reveals* (London: Christian Research, 2000).

18. Alister E. McGrath, *The Future of Christianity* (Malden, Mass.: Blackwell Publishers, 2002), 65.

19. A core competency is a unique attribute of an organization, administered with such passion and effectiveness that people both within and without the church recognize that this church has a fundamental capability and proficiency in this area.

20. Rodney Clapp, *Families at the Crossroads: Beyond Traditional and Modern Options* (Downers Grove, Ill.: InterVarsity Press, 1993), 90.

21. McGavran and Arn, *How to Grow a Church,* 115.

22. Whitesel, *Growth by Accident,* 145-46. Here I list several criteria for creating small groups in your church based upon organic interests, subcultures, and needs of the congregants rather than based upon the more customary nonorganic method of small group conscription by age and geographic proximity.

23. To address this malady, I have graphed the essential steps needed to determine if you have enough small groups to create a cohesive and organic infrastructure, in the chapter "Missteps with Small Groups" in *Growth by Accident,* 133-51.

4. The Bridge, Phoenix, Tempe, and Scottsdale, Arizona

1. Donald R. McGavran, *Understanding Church Growth* (Grand Rapids, Mich.: William B. Eerdmans Publishing Company, 1970), 395.

2. C. Peter Wagner, *Frontiers in Missionary Strategy* (Chicago: Moody Press, 1971), 123.

3. McGavran, *Understanding Church Growth,* 395.

4. Matthew 28:18-20 is called the Great Commission, for it is Christ's most succinct and tactical directive to his followers. Within this commission, four verbs are found: "go," "make disciples," "baptizing," and "teaching." Yet, in the Greek, three of these verbs have spellings that indicate they are participles, or helping verbs that further clarify a central verb. The three participles are "go," "baptizing," and "teaching." Subsequently, Jesus' choice of words reveals that the goal of our going, baptizing, and teaching is "making disciples." And due to its active tense, it may be best translated "active learners." Making active learners is thus an intended objective of Great Commission efforts.

5. C. Peter Wagner, *Church Growth and the Whole Gospel: A Biblical Mandate* (New York: Harper & Row, 1981), 13.

6. Bob Whitesel, *Growth By Accident, Death By Planning: How Not to Kill a Growing Congregation* (Nashville: Abingdon Press, 2004), 17-29, "Missteps with Staff Influence."

7. There are important parallels here with Abraham Maslow's hierarchy of needs (*Motivation and Personality,* 3rd ed. [New York: Harper & Row, 1987]). Maslow suggested that we are motivated by whatever lowest needs are currently unfulfilled. Thus, if a person's biological need such as for food, or a safety need such as for a safe place to live, are unfulfilled, they will have little interest in meeting higher needs of belonging, such as to a fellowship of believers. Therefore, Maslow's hierarchy reminds us that fulfilling the cultural mandate is part of the foundational process for meeting basic needs and eventually allows those we serve to consider higher needs for kinship.

8. In early forms, this model was first suggested by Viggo Sogaard, a student in the Wheaton Graduate School. It later was revised by James F. Engel and published in such sources as *Church Growth Bulletin* (eventually *Strategies for Today's Leader* magazine) and elsewhere during 1973. Insights on this model have been advanced by Richard Senzig of the communications faculty at the

Wheaton Graduate School and C. Peter Wagner and Charles Kraft of the Fuller School of World Mission. For more information, see James F. Engel and H. Wilbert Norton, *What's Gone Wrong with the Harvest: A Communication Strategy for the Church and World Evangelism* (Grand Rapids: Zondervan Press, 1975), 45.

9. ©Dr. Bob Whitesel, 2005. Many potential disciples have been rendered a disservice because a church focused too much on the point of conversion and not on the processes that go on before or afterward. Thus, potential disciples may have been abandoned in the process either too soon or too early because the dynamic process of Engle's model was not grasped.

10. Eddie Gibbs, *ChurchNext: Quantum Changes in How We Do Ministry* (Downers Grove, Ill.: InterVarsity Press, 2000), 231.

11. Sherwood Eliot Wirt, *The Social Conscience of the Evangelical* (New York: Harper & Row, 1968), 50.

12. Tom Sine, *Mustard Seed vs. McWorld: Reinventing Life and Faith for the Future* (Grand Rapids, Mich.: Baker Books, 1999), 225.

13. Wirt, *Social Conscience of the Evangelical,* 51.

14. A few of the many Christian agencies meeting the physical and spiritual needs of the poor, and which can serve as models and conduits for local churches, include: World Vision, World Relief, World Concern, the Salvation Army, and Samaritan's Purse, among others.

15. Wirt, *Social Conscience of the Evangelical,* 51.

5. Vintage Faith, Santa Cruz, California

1. Jean-Francois Lyotard, *The Postmodern Condition: A Report on Knowledge* (Minneapolis, Minn.: University of Minnesota Press, 1997), xxiv.

2. This multipurpose gymnasium featured basketball courts, a stage recessed into one wall, and a cheery if somewhat industrial ambiance. Such boomer predilection for light, airy, and multiuse sacred spaces seems a reaction to the builder generation's stained glass, dark wood, and inflexible worship venues.

3. Vintage Faith's goal is to have a ministry center near downtown Santa Cruz and to rent a larger worship gathering space. However, during my visit they were doing a remarkably adept job at creating a sacred space in a gymnasium.

4. Dan Kimball, www.vintagechurch.org/about.html, 2005.

5. Ibid.

6. "Ancient-future" describes the integration of historic worship features and symbols with modern elements to foster an appreciation for both historical as well as modern aspects of Christianity. By doing so, the organic church provides a bridge over which younger generations can connect to the durability and legacy of the Christian faith. The nexus of ancient-future will be investigated further in our chapter on Church of the Apostles, chap. 7.

7. To emphasize this mandate, many churches have changed the title of Minister of Music to Minister of Creative Arts. Although this is constructive, these individuals must be trained in pan-artistic forms instead of primarily in music, or they may unintentionally revert to an emphasis on music. Vintage Faith avoids this by distinguishing between a Pastor of Musical Worship and their

Director of Worship Arts. However, stronger programs in pan-artistic expression are warranted in both universities and continuing education programs.

8. In *A House Divided: Bridging the Generation Gaps in Your Church* (Nashville: Abingdon Press, 2000), Kent R. Hunter and I map out a plan for almost any church to grow into a healthy Multi-gen. congregation.

9. Adapted from the Vintage Faith Church bulletin, June 5, 2005. For exhaustive ideas for creating sacred space, see Dan Kimball's helpful book written with David Crowder and Sally Morgenthaler, titled *Emerging Worship: Creating Worship Gatherings for New Generations* (Grand Rapids, Mich.: Zondervan, 2004).

10. See chap. 3, "Missteps with Prayer," in Bob Whitesel, *Growth by Accident, Death by Planning: How Not to Kill a Growing Congregation* (Nashville: Abingdon Press, 2004), 43-53.

11. Margaret Mead, *Culture and Commitment: A Study of the Generation Gap* (Garden City, N.Y.: Natural History Press, 1970), 2.

12. Whitesel and Hunter, *A House Divided*, 98.

13. Ibid., 105-237.

6. Freeway, Baton Rouge, Louisiana

1. David Harvey, *The Condition of Postmodernity: An Enquiry into the Origins of Cultural Change* (Cambridge, Mass.: Blackwell Publishers, 1989), 62-63.

2. Paul Hiebert, *Cultural Anthropology* (Grand Rapids, Mich.: Baker Books, 1983), 25.

3. Bob Whitesel, *Growth by Accident, Death by Planning: How Not to Kill a Growing Congregation* (Nashville: Abingdon Press, 2004), 26.

4. H. Richard Niebuhr, *Christ and Culture* (New York: Harper & Brothers, 1951), 45-229. The second view is beyond the scope of our discussion. Labeled by Niebuhr "Christ of culture," it was embraced by early gnostic heretics. They interpreted Christ through cultural trends, rejecting any claims of Christ that conflicted with their culture. Counter to this, Isaiah 55:8 reminds us that God's thoughts are not our thoughts, or our ways his ways.

5. Charles H. Kraft, *Christianity in Culture: A Study in Dynamic Biblical Theologizing in Cross-Cultural Perspective* (Maryknoll, N.Y.: Orbis Books, 1979), 105-6.

6. Ibid., 108-15. Kraft sees five subdivisions of the "Christ above Culture" position. However, for this discussion only three are required. The reader seeking more exhaustive insights will benefit from a careful exploration of Kraft's work.

7. Mike Yaconelli, *Messy Spirituality: God's Annoying Love for Imperfect People* (Grand Rapids, Mich.: Zondervan, 2002). Yaconelli's viewpoint has been popular among postmodern Christians. And before his untimely death, Yaconelli was in demand as a lecturer. Young people often saw in his perspective one more in keeping with their untidy journey toward discipleship. To understand the angst and anxiety many young people sense today between their Christian understanding and their vacillating demeanor, see Yaconelli's insightful volume.

8. Kraft, *Christianity in Culture*, 113.

9. Ibid., 114.

10. Eddie Gibbs, *I Believe in Church Growth* (Grand Rapids, Mich.: William B. Eerdmans, 1981), 92.

11. In my travels through the organic church, I found its leaders usually approached the rejection or affirmation of cultural elements in a circumspect and serious manner. Whether it was the "discothèque clubbers" of England who had to decide at what point youthful fashions became lewd, or the film clips that Freeway employed to illustrate a point. Young organic leaders typically see the rejection of base elements of culture as not only required, but also judicious.

7. Church of the Apostles, Seattle, Washington

1. Harvey Cox, "Whatever Happened to Theology?" *Christianity and Crisis,* vol. 35 (1975): 114-15.

2. Karen Ward, *Worship*, www.apostleschurch.org, 2005.

3. Some feel retaining liturgical expressions can be too formulaic. And liturgy may succumb to this when it is lifted verbatim from other sources because of lack of preparation or lack of enthusiasm. However, at COTA, each aspect of a historical liturgy was present but was accompanied by modern artistic expressions. The result was a vividly engaging liturgy, which never became boring or banal.

4. First Corinthians 12 lists *apostle* as a spiritual gift. However, C. Peter Wagner has suggested an important distinction between spiritual gifts and Christian *roles* (*Your Spiritual Gifts Can Help Your Church Grow* [Ventura, Calif.: Regal Books, 1994], 85-87). Wagner sees *gifts* as extraordinary God-given skills. But he also sees Christian *roles* that parallel the gifts. For example, someone might have the supernatural *gift* of intercessory prayer and be able to pray effectively. But everyone has the *role* of praying. Thus, while the *gift* of apostle might be reserved for someone supernaturally imbued with interdenominational leadership (Wagner, *Your Spiritual Gifts,* 182), COTA stresses the apostolic *role* that all Christians have of being competently sent forth into mission.

5. Karen Ward, *About*, www.apostleschurch.org, 2005.

6. Simon Blackburn, *Truth: A Guide* (Oxford: Oxford University Press, 2005).

7. The chart is not meant to be exhaustive. It is presented here simply to give the reader a general direction of the ancient-future nexus. The elements of these columns will continue to evolve and adjust along with culture, experimentation, and effectiveness.

8. "Native" is a word I have introduced into the organic discussion due to a sense that it conveys the duality of the organic church's sentiments, in which feelings of opposite extremes are acknowledged and even expected as the result of humanity's fall. Thus, "native" sums up the dual yet inborn nature of humanness, in which emotional pairings such as the following contest with one another: for example, love-hatred, impartiality-prejudice, acceptance-alienation,

faith-doubt, community-isolation, exuberance-despondency, reassurance-apprehension, chance-predetermination, and so on. Such human duality is often expressed in the organic church's liturgy, songs, and teachings and has biblical precedence in the psalmists' meditations, for example, in Psalm 12, 53, and 139, among others.

9. Niebuhr, *Christ and Culture* (New York: Harper & Row, 1951), 45-82.

10. Charles H. Kraft, *Christianity in Culture: A Study in Dynamic Biblical Theologizing in Cross-Cultural Perspective* (Maryknoll, N.Y.: Orbis Books, 2003), 113-15.

11. Eddie Gibbs, *I Believe in Church Growth* (Grand Rapids, Mich.: William B. Eerdmans, 1981), 92-95, 120.

12. Niebuhr, *Christ and Culture,* 56. It should be noted that I have not witnessed any societal withdrawal due to monastic tendencies in the organic church. Rather, their monastic elements are primarily evident in spiritual disciplines and in elements such as praying at the monastic hours.

13. Kraft, *Christianity in Culture,* 315-27.

14. Gibbs, *I Believe in Church Growth,* 365.

15. Likewise, if a person met Christ in a Holiness revival, he or she may prefer more musical and oratory spontaneity. It is more churches who brave the ancient-future frontier that may be needed today.

16. C. Peter Wagner, *Church Growth and the Whole Gospel: A Biblical Mandate* (New York: Harper & Row, 1981), 54-57. The house diagram is adapted from C. Peter Wagner, "Principles and Procedures of Church Growth: American Church Growth," a lectureship given at Fuller Theological Seminary, Pasadena, California, January 31–February 11, 1983.

17. I have illustrated the interrelationship between the evangelical and cultural mandates in the chapter on The Bridge in Phoenix. And we will also see it exemplified in Maslow's Hierarchy of Needs later at Scum of the Earth Church in Denver.

18. W. E. Vine, *An Expository Dictionary of New Testament Words,* vol. 4 (Grand Rapids, Mich.: Fleming H. Revell Company, 1981), 179. See also Acts 18:4 and 2 Corinthians 5:11 for the use of *peitho.* And in Acts 26:28, King Agrippa uses this word to describe Paul's persuasiveness.

19. Vintage Faith Church captures this concept by referring to its congregants as theologians, but the designation may be too narrow, limiting what is designated to those primarily on the third floor. COTA, however, employs the term "apostle," which may be a better descriptor, for it conveys the outward focus of those who reside on all floors.

20. Eddie Gibbs labels a portion of this process *reciprocation,* explaining "the reciprocal relationship embodies two-way communication, with each open to be influenced by the other. Through such cross-cultural pollination the ideas of each are challenged, affirmed, enriched or modified" (*I Believe in Church Growth,* 108).

8. One Place, Phoenix, Arizona

1. Charles H. Kraft, *Christianity in Culture: A Study in Dynamic Biblical Theologizing in Cross-Cultural Perspective* (Maryknoll, N.Y.: Orbis Books, 2003), 318.

2. Though One Place met in a school auditorium of an affluent suburb, their focus in music, word, and ministry has always been the inner city. No degree of modern accruements could mask this.

3. *Bulletin,* January 23, 2005. According to Mark Roberts, these guiding values were created by the staff after a late-night brainstorming session.

4. The term "stations" is often applied to these artistic interactivities. This is drawn from the historical Christian practice of using fourteen or fifteen Stations of the Cross as reminders of Jesus' passion and resurrection (the fifteenth). The organic church employs this term in part because of proficiency, but also because of its historical connection.

5. Vintage Faith Church in Santa Cruz is a congregation that is especially adroit at this.

6. George G. Hunter, *The Celtic Way of Evangelism: How Christianity Can Reach the West . . . Again* (Nashville: Abingdon Press, 2000), 74.

7. Adapted from Fred R. David, *Strategic Management: Concepts and Cases,* 9th ed. (Upper Saddle River, N.J.: Prentice Hall, 2003), 61.

8. Based upon Sy Landau, Barbara Landau, and Daryl Landau, *From Conflict to Creativity: How Resolving Workplace Disagreements Can Inspire Innovation and Productivity* (San Francisco: Jossey-Bass, 2001), 128-29 and adapted from Bob Whitesel, *Growth by Accident, Death by Planning: How Not to Kill a Growing Congregation* (Nashville: Abingdon Press, 2004), 91.

9. Gareth R. Jones, Jennifer M. George, and Charles W. L. Hill, *Contemporary Management,* 2nd ed. (Boston: McGraw-Hill, 2000), 217.

10. Andrew Campbell and Sally Yeung, "Creating a Sense of Mission," *Long Range Planning,* 24, no. 4 (August, 1991): 17.

9. Scum of the Earth Church, Denver, Colorado

1. Nirvana, *Nevermind,* Geffen Records, 1991.

2. Winston Churchill, *Time* (New York, September 12, 1960).

3. For more information on how facilities can thwart church growth, see chap. 5, "Missteps with New Facilities," in Bob Whitesel, *Growth by Accident, Death by Planning: How Not To Kill a Growing Congregation* (Nashville: Abingdon Press, 2004), 73-83.

4. In *A House Divided: Bridging the Generation Gaps in Your Church* (Nashville: Abingdon Press, 2000), Kent R. Hunter and I pointed out that a generational predilection for different artistic expressions in worship is a byproduct of a market-driven economy in which advertisers segment the market into affinity sectors. Everything from cars, colas, cameras, and computers are targeted toward different age groups. The outcome has been a distinct preference by each generation for different artistic expressions, primarily in music, but also in ambiance. Churches that desire to reach more than one generation will need to be flexible in their facilities as well as the ambiance they employ.

5. For seven steps toward growing an organic Multi-gen. church, see Bob Whitesel and Kent R. Hunter, *A House Divided.*

6. Adapted from Abraham H. Maslow, *Motivation and Personality,* 2nd ed.

(New York: Harper & Row, 1970), 300-394; and Abraham H. Maslow, *The Farther Reaches of Human Nature,* (New York: Viking Press, 1971), 300.

7. For more information on the interrelationship between the evangelistic and the cultural mandates, see the chapter on The Bridge of Phoenix, as well as the Finale of this book.

8. Carl C. H. Henry, "Postmodernism: The New Spectre" in *The Challenge of Postmodernism: An Evangelical Engagement,* ed. David S. Dockery (Wheaton, Ill.: Victor Books, 1995), 48-51.

9. Ibid., 48-49.

10. Ibid., 48.

11. George G. Hunter, *The Celtic Way of Evangelism: How Christianity Can Reach the West...Again* (Nashville: Abingdon Press, 2000), 97.

12. C. Peter Wagner, *On the Crest of the Wave: Becoming a World Christian* (Ventura, Calif.: Regal Books, 1983), 112. Wagner states, "The obvious lesson for missionary strategy is that the seed of the Word must be concentrated on the fertile soil if fruit is to be expected. Some peoples of the world are receptive to the gospel while others are resistant. The world's fertile soils should be tested before sowing the seed" (p. 112).

13. Donald A. McGavran, *Understanding Church Growth* (Grand Rapids, Mich.: William B. Eerdmans, 1970), 262.

14. Paul Hiebert, *Cultural Anthropology* (Philadelphia: J. B. Lippincott, 1976), 25.

15. Ibid., 121. Also see Eugene Nida's examination of cultural signs and symbols in *Message and Mission: The Communication of the Christian Faith* (South Pasadena, Calif.: Willliam Carey Library, 1975), 65.

10. Bluer, Minneapolis, Minnesota

1. George Barna, *The Index of Leading Spiritual Indicators* (Dallas: Word Publishers, 1996), 50.

2. Charismatic or neo-Pentecostal are designations used to describe evangelical churches that hold to a modified form of classical Pentecostal theology. William G. MacDonald describes classical Pentecostals as a "segment of the body of Christ that ardently proclaims that Pentecost is *repeatable*" (*Perspectives on the New Pentecostalism,* ed. Russell P. Spittler [Grand Rapids, Mich.: Baker Book House, 1976], 59). Customarily, charismatics concur with classical Pentecostals that the more remarkable gifts of the Holy Spirit such as speaking in tongues and prophetic utterances are valid and helpful gifts for the church to use today. Charismatics often digress from their classical brethren by either remaining in their mainline churches, denying that speaking in tongues is the initial and dominant evidence of the baptism in the Holy Spirit, and/or aligning with new transcongregational networks.

3. John Musick, *Bluer: Seek the Deep,* n.d.

4. James D. G. Dunn, *Jesus and the Spirit: A Study of the Religious and Charismatic Experience of Jesus and the First Christians as Reflected in the New Testament* (Philadelphia: Westminster Press, 1975), 357-58.

5. John Musick, *2005 Bluer Focus,* n.d.

6. For a complete step-by-step explanation of how most churches can grow into multigenerational congregations, see *A House Divided: Bridging the Generation Gaps in Your Church* (Nashville: Abingdon Press, 2000), 105-237. In this volume, I explain how churches can develop into a multigenerational model by following these steps: (1) learn about the strengths of the Multi-gen. model, (2) create new multigenerational leadership structures, (3) identify the needs of the unchurched, (4) create parallel worship options, (5) befriend and invite expansively and extensively, (6) evaluate your success continually, and (7) mobilize your church for multigenerational prayer.

7. According to John 16:8-9, only the Holy Spirit can convict of sin, call to repentance, and convert people to Christ.

8. Eddie Gibbs, *I Believe in Church Growth* (Grand Rapids, Mich.: William B. Eerdmans, 1981), 188.

9. See chap. 10, "Step 6: Evaluate Your Success" (pp. 202-21), in *A House Divided*, by Whitesel and Hunter; and chap. 7, "Missteps with Evaluation" (pp. 97-107), in *Growth by Accident Death, by Planning: How Not to Kill a Growing Congregation*, by Bob Whitesel (Nashville: Abingdon Press, 2004).

11. Tribe of Los Angeles, Los Angeles, California

1. Theodor W. Adorno, *The Culture Industry: Selected Essays on Mass Culture*, 2nd ed. (New York: Routledge, 2001), 67.

2. Ibid.

3. Drumming is often associated with world music, which reflects the rich diversity of musical expression found in nonwestern cultures. The Tribe's parallels with sub-Saharan music are brought out in Roger Kamien's observation that in that region, "music is a social activity in which almost everyone participates. It is usually performed outdoors, and there is spontaneous music making as well as performances by social and music groups at ceremonies and feasts. There is no musical notation; musical tradition, like folklore and history is transmitted orally" (*Music: An Appreciation*, 3rd ed. [New York: McGraw-Hill, 1984], 388).

4. As director of the Los Angeles Film Study Center, Ver Straten-McSparran is sensitive to video and film clips being used out of context. Thus, she prefers to use longer segments of videos or movies to preserve their context. In addition, she only employs clips whose message is consistent with the film or video's overall ethos, believing too often the message conveyed can be opposed to the creators' intentions.

5. Using natural theology, a sermonizer might expound upon the miracles of the universe, the wonders of the heavens, the laws of physics, and then inductively suggest that there is a Master Designer behind it. Often with natural theology, the evidence is stated, but the principle behind it must be logically thought through by the listener. In this case, the listener should conclude that there is a designer, behind the design. This argument, called the Teleological Argument, is based upon the listener using his or her own intellect to draw theological conclusions, rather than the teacher drawing the conclusions for the listener.

6. After reading my journeys through the organic church, the reader will notice that postmodern generations are more open to arguments based on

151

natural theology than they are open to those based on revealed theology. The questioning, discussion, and even argumentative exchanges that characterize organic sermons are often evidence of natural theology taking place. This often indicates that the answers are not being spoon-fed to listeners, but that the speaker trusts in the logical, analytical, and rational mind that God has given the listeners to induce the validity of God's principles. Thus, natural theology often begins with concepts and evidence and then works backward in an inductive way to a rational and biblical explanation.

7. I employ a capital "t" when referring to the Truth to designate what I believe to be legitimate and authentic Truth as revealed in God's Word. However, in employing this symbolic convention, I am making a statement that not all organic churches would agree with, though in my experience most would.

8. Donald A. McGavran, *Understanding Church Growth* (Grand Rapids: William B. Eerdmans, 1970), 295-313.

9. In *Growth by Accident, Death by Planning: How Not To Kill a Growing Congregation* (Nashville: Abingdon Press, 2004), I have devoted a chapter on how to remain connected to those you seek to reach. I have discovered that a distancing of leaders physically and emotionally to their mission field is one of the eleven most common causes of church attendance plateaus. For ten corrective steps, see chap. 1, "Missteps with Staff Influence," on pages 17-29.

12. Solomon's Porch, Minneapolis, Minnesota

1. Michiko Kakutani, "Art Is Easier the Second Time Around," *New York Time* (October 30, 1994): E-4.

2. Doug Pagitt and the Solomon's Porch Community, *Reimagining Spiritual Formation: A Week in the Life of an Experimental Church* (Grand Rapids, Mich.: Zondervan, 2003), 136.

3. Regrettably, those leading worship gatherings do not usually notice incipient boredom. One of my students pointed out that pastors are so often caught up in a sermon that time seems to fly. But unfortunately, those in the pew often do not experience this same elation.

4. The institutional feel of many boomer sanctuaries inhibits discussion, and as such dialogue is often relegated to increasingly large foyers and narthexes. However, the comfortable living room environment of the organic church brings conversation and personal ministry back into the sanctuary.

5. Pagitt, *Reimagining Spiritual Formation,* 137.

6. Ibid., 52.

7. *Solomon's Porch,* n.d. The congregation's name comes from Acts 5:12-13, which this pamphlet paraphrases as: "All the believers used to meet together at Solomon's Porch . . . the people thought highly of them."

8. This living room ambiance is intended "to make the things of God seem normal . . . to create a normal place that gives us permission to discuss the unique things of God" (Pagitt, *Reimagining Spiritual Formation,* 53).

9. Ibid., 132.

10. Ibid., 132-33. Here, Pagitt also argues that creativity becomes a powerful

tool for spiritual formation and discipleship. See Pagitt's insightful tome for an extended treatise on the nexus of creativity and spiritual formation.

11. Charles Kraft, *Christianity in Culture: A Study in Dynamic Biblical Theologizing in Cross-Cultural Perspective* (Maryknoll, N.Y.: Orbis Books, 2003), 113-15.

12. Ibid., 382.

13. Alan Roxburgh, "Missional Leadership: Equipping God's People for Mission," in *Missional Church: A Vision for the Sending of the Church in North America,* ed. Darrell Guder (Grand Rapids, Mich.: William B. Eerdmans Publishing Company, 1998), 205-8.

14. *Lectio divina* is a slow, contemplative prayer discipline, during which selected scriptures form the basis for personal reflection and application. A Christian monastic tradition, it includes a leisurely oscillation back and forth between scripture, meditation, prayer, and personal application. In today's hectic world and church life, such unhurried reflection can be refreshing. A good small group study guide that can introduce your congregation to *lectio* is *Listening for God Through 1 & 2 Peter* by Time Guptill (Kansas City: Beacon Press, 2006).

15. A young man who was a trained drummer told Pagitt that he disliked drum circles, "for it gives people who are not drummers a drum to beat." To this Pagitt replied with a customary emphasis on the importance of the leadership-followership experience: "As a preacher, I think it's like giving everyone their own Bible." His point was well made.

16. Some organic readers may take umbrage with my inclusion of a management writer in this book on organic structures. However, Mary Parker Follette has defined management as "the art of getting things done through people" (quoted in James A. F. Stoner, *Management,* 2nd ed. [Englewood Cliff, N.J.: 1982], 7). In this regard, the organic church may be doing a better job than the nonorganic boomer church. In fact, this was one of my premises in the first two chapters of this book, in which organic was chosen as a befitting appellation because the postmodern church is doing a better job than the boomer church in attaining pervasive involvement in ministry.

17. Peter Drucker, *Managing for Results: Economic Tasks and Risk-taking Decisions* (New York: Harper & Row, 1964), 5.

18. Franky Schaeffer, *Addicted to Mediocrity: 20th Century Christians and the Arts* (Westchester, Ill.: Crossway Books, 1981).

19. Darrell L. Guder, *Be My Witnesses: The Church's Mission, Message, and Messengers* (Grand Rapids, Mich.: William B. Eerdmans, 1985),182-90. In this book, Guder develops a convincing argument for the metaphorical use of "tabernacle" rather than "temple" when describing a church engaged in reaching a culture.

20. Drucker, *Managing for Results,* 5.

21. Viola Spolin, *Improvisation for the Theater: A Handbook of Teaching and Directing Techniques,* 3rd ed. (Evanston, Ill.: Northwestern University Press, 1999), 299.

22. Ibid., 26.

23. Gary Hamel and Peter Skarzynski, *On Creativity, Innovation, and Renewal: A Leader to Leader Guide,* ed. Frances Hesselbein and Rob Johnston (San Francisco: Jossey-Bass, 2002), 13-14.
24. Ibid., 13.
25. Guder, *Be My Witnesses,* 182-90.

13. Nurturing an Organic Congregation: The Leadership Collage

1. Mary Jo Hatch, *Organization Theory: Modern, Symbolic, and Postmodern Perspectives* (Oxford: Oxford University Press, 1997), 53.
2. Mary Jo Hatch, Monika Kostera, and Andrzej K. Kozminski, *The Three Faces of Leadership: Manager, Artist, Priest* (Malden, Mass.: Blackwell Publishing, 2005), vii.
3. Ed Setzer, *Planting New Churches in a Postmodern Age* (Nashville: Broadman & Holman Publishers, 2003), 137.
4. For an understanding of the organizational structure of churches as *congregation-subcongregation-cell,* see Bob Whitesel and Kent R. Hunter, *A House Divided: Bridging the Generation Gaps in Your Church* (Nashville: Abingdon Press, 2001), 25-30.
5. Phil Stevenson in *The Ripple Church: Multiplying Your Ministry by Parenting New Churches* ([Indianapolis: Wesleyan Publishing, 2004], 54-59) identifies nine models of church parenting, including daughtering, shared parenting, multi-campuses, colonization, the restart, language group congregations, inside-out planting, house churches, and the next paradigm model.
6. Mary Jo Hatch, *Organization Theory,* 53.
7. Ibid.
8. Ibid., 54.
9. For a comprehensive look at the factors that comprise an organization's external environment, see Fred R. David, *Strategic Management: Concepts and Cases,* 9th ed. (Upper Saddle River, N.J.: Prentice Hall, 2003), 80-112.
10. Bob Whitesel, *Staying Power: Why People Leave the Church Over Change and What You Can Do About It* (Nashville: Abingdon Press, 2003).
11. Mary Jo Hatch, *Organization Theory,* 53.
12. Ibid., 48.
13. Quoted by Fred R. David, *Strategic Management,* 301.